W9-ADR-918

Environmental Science

Disclaimer

Adult supervision is required when working on these projects. No responsibility is implied or taken for anyone who sustains injuries as a result of using the materials or ideas, or performing the procedures put forth in this book. Use proper equipment (gloves, forceps, safety glasses, etc.) and take other safety precautions such as tying up loose hair and clothing and washing your hands when the work is done. Use extra care with chemicals, dry ice, boiling water, or any heating elements. Hazardous chemicals and live cultures (organisms) must be handled and disposed of according to appropriate directions set forth by your (adult advisor). Follow your science fair's rules and regulations and/or the standard scientific practices and procedures set forth by your school or other governing body.

Additional safety precautions and warnings are mentioned throughout the text. If you use common sense and make safety a first consideration, you will create a safe, fun, educational, and rewarding project.

Environmental Science

High school science fair experiments

H. Steven Dashefsky
Illustrations by Janice Lebeyka

TAB Books
Division of McGraw-Hill, Inc.
Blue Ridge Summit, PA 17294-0850

GE77 . D38   1994

©1994 by **TAB Books**.
Published by TAB Books, a division of McGraw-Hill, Inc.

Printed in the United States of America. All rights reserved. The publisher
takes no responsibility for the use of any materials or methods described in this
book, nor for the products thereof.

1 2 3 4 5 6 7 8 9 0 FGR/FGR 9 9 8 7 6 5 4

Library of Congress Cataloging-in-Publication Data
Dashefsky, H. Steven.
   Environmental science : high-school science fair projects / by
H. Steven Dashefsky
     p.   cm.
   Includes index.
   ISBN 0-8306-4587-X   ISBN 0-8306-4586-1 (pbk.)
   1. Environmental sciences—Study and teaching (Higher)—Activity
programs. 2. Science projects. [1. Environmental sciences-
-Experiments. 2. Experiments. 3. Science projects.] I. Title.
GE77.D38   1993
574.5'078—dc20   93-34615
                                                         CIP
                                                          AC

Acquisitions Editor: Kim Tabor
Editorial team: Joanne Slike, Supervising Editor
               Marianne Krcma, Book Editor
Production team: Katherine G. Brown, Director
               Ollie Harmon, Coding
               Rose McFarland, Layout
               Cindi Bell, Proofreading
               Joann Woy, Indexer
Design team: Jaclyn J. Boone, Designer
            Brian Allison, Associate Designer
Cover design: Sandra Blair Design, Harrisburg, Pa.   GEN1
Cover photography: Bender and Bender Photography, Waldo, Ohio   4515

Acknowledgments

Many of the projects in this book were adapted from original International Science and Engineering Fairs (ISEF) award-winning projects. I want to thank the following students for these outstanding projects and wish them the best of luck in their future scientific endeavors:

- Lisa Parker for "Bug Lights: More Harm Than Good?" (chapter 4)
- Amanda Cowart for "Plant Stimulation and Growth" (chapter 12)
- Robert Sammons for "Wind Power: An Alternative to Fossil Fuels" (chapter 14)
- Nidhi Gupta for "Electromagnetic Radiation: Our Silent Partner" (chapter 15)

I'd also like to thank my friend and colleague, Mr. Skip Kilmer, from the Greenhill School in Dallas for "Solar Energy: An Alternative to Fossil Fuels" (chapter 13). Thanks to Roger Cox at Save the Planet Software for his assistance with "Computer Modeling & the Hole in the Ozone Layer" (chapter 8) and to George Reid and Jerry Freeman at Fairfield Engineering for their assistance with "Electromagnetic Radiation & Personal Computers" (chapter 16).

Finally, thanks to the following people for their technical assistance with many of the other projects: Olga Slobobkina, Christina Ramirez, and Kim Youngsworth, all from Marymount College in Tarrytown, New York, and Carolyn Bardwell and Vincent D'Amico at the University of Massachusetts in Amherst.

Contents

How to use this book   **x**

A word about safety & supervision   **xiii**

Part 1
Before you begin

1 An introduction to environmental science   **2**
Environment   *2*
Ecology   *3*
Environmental science   *3*
Our environment—What's going on?   *4*
Ecological studies   *6*

2 An introduction to scientific research   **8**
The scientific method   *9*
Building on past science fair projects   *11*

3 Getting started   **12**
Use this book   *12*
Other sources   *12*
Talk to specialists in the field   *13*
Put your signature on the project   *13*
Before you begin   *14*
Performing the experiment   *14*

Part 2
Applied ecology

4 Bug lights: More harm than good? **20**

5 Waxed fruit:
What you see is not what you get **26**

6 Composting goes high-tech **34**

7 Cleaning up oil spills:
Bioremediation **42**

8 Computer modeling &
the hole in the ozone layer **49**

Part 3
Soil ecosystems

9 Earthworms & humus **60**

10 Environmental stress & earthworms **66**

11 Nitrogen fixation & acid rain **72**

12 Plant stimulation & growth **77**

Part 4
Energy: For better & for worse

13 Solar energy:
An alternative to fossil fuels **86**

14 Wind power:
An alternative to fossil fuels **92**

15 Electromagnetic radiation:
   Our silent partner   **100**

16 Electromagnetic radiation &
   personal computers   **106**

Part 5
Aquatic ecosystems

17 Heavy metal contamination: Synergism   **114**

18 Fertilizer, sewage &
   aquatic ecosystems   **121**

19 Acid rain & algae   **128**

20 Nutrient-enriched waters & algae   **135**

Part 6
New solutions to old problems

21 Biocontrol: Predators, parasites,
   & parasitoids   **144**

22 Parasitoids: Behavior & pest control   **153**

23 Ice-nucleating bacteria: Let it rain   **157**

A Using metrics   **163**

B Sources   **165**

   Glossary   **171**

   Index   **175**

   About the author   **178**

How to use this book

There are two ways to use this book. If you are new to science fair projects and feel that you need a great deal of technical guidance, you can use the projects as explained in this book with little or no adjustment. These are good, solid science fair projects. However, if you want to be a contender for an award-winning project, you must use the experiments in the book as the foundation only, incorporating your own additional ideas into the project. Many suggestions for how to do this are given in the "Going further" or "Suggested research" sections of each project. This book is designed to provide core experiments with many suggestions about how to expand the scope or adjust the focus of each experiment.

Each project in this book has the following sections:
- Background
- Project overview
- Materials list
- Procedures
- Analysis
- Going further
- Suggested research

Background

The "Background" section provides information about the topic to be investigated. It offers you a frame of reference so you can see the importance of the topic and why research is necessary to advance our understanding. This section could be considered the initial step in your literature search. Although a small step, reading this section is enough to see if the subject interests you.

Project overview

If the "Background" section interests you, continue reading because the "Project overview" section describes the purpose of the project. It explains the problems that exist and poses questions that the experiment is intended to resolve. These questions can be used to formulate your hypothesis. Be sure to discuss this section and the next with your sponsor to see if the requirements imposed can realistically be met.

Materials list

The "Materials list" explains everything you need to perform the experiment. Be sure you have access to or can get everything before beginning. Some pieces of equipment are expensive. Check with your teacher to see if all the equipment is available in your school or if it can be borrowed from elsewhere. Be sure your budget can handle anything that must be purchased. A list of scientific supply houses is provided at the back of the book.

Although most people don't think of research scientists as being particularly good with hammers, nails, and other tools, they must be. Building a device or experimental workstation often involves many trips to the hardware store for supplies, a little sweat on the brow, and a lot of ingenuity.

Most living organisms, such as bacterial cultures, must be ordered from scientific supply houses. A few, such as insects, can be ordered, purchased locally, or caught depending on the project, your location, and the time of year. If you are using live organisms, work with your sponsor to be sure you adhere to all science fair regulations and standard biological research practices. Before beginning, discuss with your sponsor the proper way to dispose of any hazardous materials, chemicals, or cultures.

Procedures

The "Procedures" section gives step-by-step instructions on how to perform the experiment and suggestions on how to collect data. Be sure to read through this section with your sponsor before undertaking the project. Illustrations are often used to clarify procedures. Although each step is given, some projects require standard procedures such as inoculating a petri dish. These steps are often stated but not explained. Your sponsor can help you with these standard procedures.

Analysis

The "Analysis" section doesn't draw conclusions for you. Instead, it asks questions to help you analyze and interpret the data so you can come to your own conclusions. In many cases, empty tables and charts are provided for you to begin your data collection. You should convert as much of your raw data as possible into line, bar, or pie charts.

Some experiments might require statistical analysis to determine if there are significant differences between the experimental groups and the control group. Check with your sponsor to see if you should perform statistical analysis for your project, and if so, what kind. The appendix called "Further reading" in the back of this book lists books that will help you analyze your data.

Going further

"Going further" is a vital section of every project. It lists many ways for you to continue researching the topic beyond the original experiment. These suggestions can be followed as is or even more importantly, they might spark your imagination to think of some new twist or angle to take while performing the project. These suggestions may show ways to more thoroughly cover the subject matter and/or show you how to broaden the scope of the project. The best way to assure an interesting and fully developed project is to include one or more of the suggestions from the Going further section or include an idea of your own that was inspired from this section.

Suggested research

The "Suggested research" section proposes new directions to follow while researching the project. It often suggests what to read, as well as organizations, companies, and other sources to contact. Using these additional resources might turn your project into a winner.

A word about safety & supervision

All the projects in this book require an adult sponsor to ensure the student's safety and the safety of others. Science Service, Inc. is an organization that sets science fair rules, regulations, and safety guidelines and holds the International Science and Engineering Fairs (ISEF). This book recommends and assumes that students performing projects in this book follow ISEF guidelines as they pertain to adult supervision. ISEF guidelines state that students undertaking a science fair project have an Adult Sponsor assigned to them.

The *adult sponsor* is described as a teacher, parent, professor, or scientist in whose lab the student is working. (For the purpose of this book, this will usually be the student's teacher.) This person must have a solid background in science and be in close contact with the student throughout the project. The adult sponsor is responsible for the safety of the student while conducting the research, including the handling of all equipment, chemicals, and organisms. The sponsor must also be familiar with regulations and commonly approved practices that govern chemical and equipment usage, experimental techniques, the use of laboratory animals, cultures and microorganisms, and proper disposal techniques.

If the adult sponsor is not qualified to handle all of these responsibilities, the sponsor must assign other adults who can fulfill these responsibilities. Most science fairs require appropriate forms be filled out before proceeding with a project that identify the Adult Sponsor and his or her qualifications.

The sponsor is responsible for reviewing the student's Research Plan, as described later in this book, and making sure the experimentation is done within local, federal and ISEF (or other appropriate governing body's) guidelines.

The entire project should be read and reviewed by the student and the adult sponsor before beginning. The adult should determine which portions of the experiment the student can perform without supervision and which portions will require supervision. In addition, a ⚠ throughout the text indicates procedures that are potentially hazardous.

For a copy of the ISEF's rules and regulations contact Science Service, Inc. at 1719 N Street, N.W., Washington, DC 20036, (202) 785-2255. The booklet includes a checklist for the adult sponsor, approval forms, and valuable information on all aspects of participating in a science fair.

Part 1

Before you begin

Before delving into any scientific experiment, there are three things to understand: the terminology used, the methodology required, and the suitability of the project to your own situation and preferences. The following three chapters examine these elements.

1

An introduction to environmental science

Before delving into a project in environmental science, it's important to understand some basic terminology. What do the terms *environment*, *ecology*, and *environmental science* really mean?

Environment

The first thing to understand about the term *environment* is that it assumes the perspective of an organism. When talking about an environment, you are speaking about the environment of a specific organism such as the lion's, rabbit's, insect's or paramecium's environment. One organism's environment might be another organisms waste. (See Fig. 1-1.) People often use the phrase *our environment*, as in ". . . polluting our environment," in which case the term is used from our (human) perspective.

An organism's environment includes everything that surrounds that organism, which can be divided into three components. The first is the nonliving component, which includes such things as soil, air, and water. The second is the living component, which includes all other organisms that live in association with the organism in question. The final component consists of all other factors, such as temperature, humidity, and radiation.

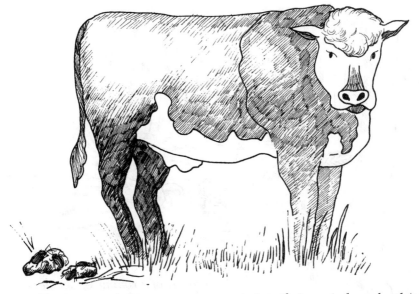

1-1 *The term* environment *assumes a point of view. A dung beetle's environment is a pile of cow manure.*

Ecology

The term *ecology* refers to the study of how these three environmental components (living, nonliving, and other factors) interact with one another. For example, the ecology of a pond refers to the study of all three components within and around that pond.

   Ecology can refer to the study of any area. For example, you could study the ecology of a rotting log, as in Fig. 1-2. This includes organisms that live on and in the log, the soil beneath the log, the moisture content and acidity of the log, and how all these factors interact. You can think of the term *environment* as a set of dominoes and *ecology* as the domino effect, or how the pieces interact with each other when they fall.

Environmental science

Finally, the term *environmental science* is used to describe how human populations and their technologies affect our planet and the global ecology of our planet. It goes beyond determining what the effects are, though, by attempting to resolve the problems once they are identified. Since global changes occur slowly, harm being done today might not begin to reveal itself for decades to come. For this

1-2
The ecology of a rotting log includes all living things (fungi, insects, etc.), nonliving things (soil and moisture) and other factors like temperature and acidity found within and around the log.

reason, it is often difficult to distinguish between real problems and those some people believe might not be problems.

For example, global warming is believed to be occurring as you read this, but we won't know for sure for many years. Can we wait until the symptoms actually show themselves before trying to resolve the problem? Unfortunately, in most cases, it will take as long for the harm to reverse itself as it took for the symptoms to appear. So waiting to be sure might be too late.

Our environment—What's going on?

Think about it. For decades people have dumped their sewage, municipal solid wastes, manufacturing wastes, radioactive wastes, and just about every other kind of garbage imaginable into streams, rivers, lakes, and oceans. Why did it take decades before people began to realize we were destroying these ecosystems? Common sense would indicate a problem might be in the making, but we didn't realize it until the Great Lakes died, hypodermic needles washed ashore on beaches along the coastline, and bodies of water everywhere began to stink.

Why do we spray billions of tons of pesticides every year when we know it contaminates our ground water supplies, is on the food we eat, and is found in some mothers' breast milk? Common sense might indicate there is a problem in the making, but we don't see the direct link between pesticides and ecological and personal health, so we hesitate to act.

Environmental scientists have a tough role to play. There are four things they must do:

1 Identify a problem.

2 Determine the problem's cause.

3 Demonstrate the link between the problem and the cause.

4 Resolve the problem.

Unfortunately, even if the first two things are accomplished, it doesn't mean anything will be done to resolve the problem. This is because most people require a demonstrable cause-and-effect link to be established, but this is sometimes difficult if not impossible to do.

Most of our environmental problems are multifaceted, and they require multifaceted solutions. For environmental scientists to accomplish the four tasks mentioned, many scientific disciplines must be integrated. Biology, chemistry, medicine, physics, agriculture, engineering, and earth and computer sciences are often involved. Many problems must also take into account economics, sociology, ethics, and philosophy. Almost all of the solutions also involve politics, finance, the law and public relations. This complexity is illustrated in Fig. 1-3.

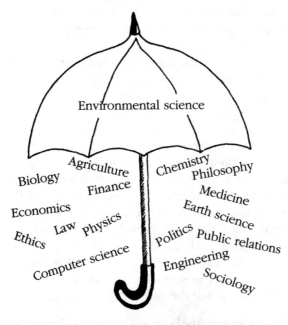

1-3 *Environmental science is a phrase that encompasses many sciences and disciplines. It integrates them all in an attempt to identify and resolve our environmental problems.*

Ecological studies

Since ecological studies are multifaceted, they can be difficult to describe. They can be described by looking at either: 1. what is being studied; 2. how it is studied; or 3. what the goal is of the study. Most scientific research does not involve just one of these aspects, but incorporates all. By understanding all the pieces, you'll have a better understanding of environmental science in its entirety.

What to study

Some studies focus on a particular habitat, such as soil or aquatic ecosystems. Studies can focus more specifically on certain types of organisms, such as plants, animals, or microbes, that live within an ecosystem. They can also focus on a specific biological system. For example, studies might be concerned with a single population, a community of populations, or an entire ecosystem.

Methods of study

Ecological research is often divided into three major categories. *Descriptive ecology* does just that—describes what is found in an ecosystem. Most early ecological studies mapped out what components existed in an ecosystem. Some of the experiments in this book have some descriptive aspects, such as "Acid Rain and Algae" and "Nutrient-Enriched Waters and Algae."

Experimental ecology focuses on the effect that changes will have on an ecosystem. These changes can be made to either the organism or (more likely) to the organism's environment. For example, what will happen to certain forms of life if acid rain falls, or ultraviolet radiation exposure increases? Many of the projects in this book fall into this category. See the projects in parts 3, 4, and 5.

Theoretical ecology also attempts to see how change affects life on our planet, but it also projects what will happen in the future. Theoretical ecology uses existing data, analyzes it, and theorizes what will happen years, decades, and centuries from now. For example, based upon the data already collected on global warming, computers can be used to project what will happen to the ice caps and sea levels in 10, 20, or 30 years. If you are interested in computers and our environment, this is the science for you. See the project entitled "Computer modeling and the hole in the ozone layer."

Pure research and applied ecology

The purpose of some research is purely to gain facts, without any concrete reason for doing so. For example, knowing the genetic makeup of a microbe, for no other reason but to know, is considered *pure research*. But pure research provides the foundation to move on to *applied research*, where you take the basic facts and make them work for you. For example, finding a gene that can make a plant resistant to drought or finding a protein that can be used to make rain are examples of applied research. (See Fig. 1-4.)

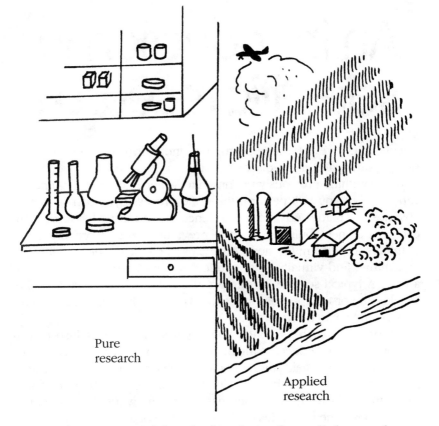

Pure research

Applied research

1-4 *Pure research lays the foundation for applied research.*

Parts 2 and 6 focus on applied ecology, including subjects such as advancing oil spill clean-ups, the potential hazards of waxed fruit, improved high-tech composting, the best way to use bug lights, biological control of insect pests, and using ice-nucleating bacteria to make it rain.

An introduction to scientific research

Science fairs give you the opportunity to not only learn about a topic, but to participate in the discovery process. You probably won't discover something previously unknown to science (although you never can tell), but you will perform the same process by which such discoveries are made. Advances in science move forward slowly, with each experiment building upon a previous one and preparing researchers to perform the next. Advances in medicine, biotechnology, agriculture, and virtually all scientific disciplines proceed one step at a time. A typical science fair project allows you to see what it is like to take one or two of these steps for yourself. The following typifies how science marches forward.

A problem such as controlling a particular type of insect pest without harmful pesticides might be solved by a series of scientific experiments. First, field studies could search for natural predators and parasites of the pest. Lab and field studies could then be performed to determine how effective each natural enemy would be at controlling the pest. The life cycles of these insects would be studied as well to see how each would fit into the local ecosystem.

Further studies might be performed to determine the population dynamics of these natural enemies. Are they capable of controlling the pest? What would happen to the entire ecosystem if the number of these predators dramatically increased by being artificially introduced?

Some experiments might find some of the enemies to be incapable of controlling the pest. Even these studies, however, are valuable because they provide information that keeps scientists on the right track. Once a natural enemy was found to be a likely candidate, small-scale testing could begin until a solution to the problem is found.

In this example, each experiment is necessary before the next can be performed, and the entire progression is necessary before a successful conclusion can be reached. Scientific research, no matter how simple or how sophisticated, must follow a protocol that demands consistency and, most important, duplication. When one scientist or research team finds some new revelation, others must verify it. The scientific method provides a framework for researchers to follow. It assures a highly focused, reproducible sequence of events. The fundamentals of the scientific method are discussed in the following pages.

The scientific method

The scientific method can be divided into five steps. The paragraphs that follow describe these steps and relate them to sections in this book.

Problem

What question do you want to answer, or what problem would you like to solve? For example, can a parasitoid wasp distinguish between good and damaged host eggs and how? Can a certain type of insect be used to control a particular pest? The "Project overview" section of each project in this book gives a number of questions and problems to think about. The "Going further" and "Suggested research" sections also give you ideas to spark your imagination about additional problems.

Hypothesis

A *hypothesis* is an educated guess, based on your literature search, that offers a possible answer to the questions posed. You might hypothesize that the wasp can distinguish between good and damaged eggs and does so by touch or that a certain type of parasite can control a particular pest. You can form a hypothesis about any or all of the questions given in the "Project overview" section.

Experimentation

The experiment is designed to determine whether the hypothesis is correct or not. Even if the hypothesis isn't correct, a well-designed experiment helps determine why it isn't correct.

There are two major parts to the experiment. The first is designing and setting up the experiment. How must you prepare the experiment and what procedures must be followed to test the hypothesis? What materials will be needed? What live organisms, if any, are needed? What step-by-step procedures must be followed during the experiment? What observations and data must be made and collected while the experiment is running? Once these questions have been answered, the actual experiment can begin.

The second part is performing the actual experiment, making observations, and collecting data. The results must be documented for study and analysis. The more details, the better. There are three important things to remember when performing research: take notes, take notes, and take notes. The most common mistake new scientists make is thinking they will remember some small detail. If you always carry a notebook and pencil when working on your project, this won't be a problem. Some science fairs require the project notebook be submitted along with a brief abstract of the project. Some fairs require or encourage a full-length report of the project, as well.

The "Materials list" section of each project indicates all the materials needed for each experiment, and the "Procedures" section gives step-by-step instructions. Suggestions are given on what observations should be made and data to be collected.

Another aspect of experimentation is the importance of replication. For any project to be considered valid scientific work, the experimental groups should be replicated as many times as are practical. The duplicated groups can then be averaged together or, better yet, statistically analyzed. For the projects in this book, try to perform all experimental groups in triplicate. For example, if you are collecting samples from a site, collect three times in the general area; if you are culturing organisms, establish three such cultures. Replication reduces the chance of collecting spurious data which will result in incorrect analysis and conclusions.

Analysis

Once you have completed the experiment and collected the data, you must analyze it and draw conclusions to determine if your hypothesis was correct. Create tables, charts or graphs to help analyze the data. The "Procedures" section of each project suggests what observations to make and data to collect while running the experiment. The "Analysis" section asks important questions to help you analyze the data and often contains empty tables or charts to fill in with your data. This book provides guidance, but you must draw your own conclusions. "Suggested reading" in Appendix B lists other books to help you analyze data.

The conclusions should be based upon your original hypothesis. Was it correct? Even if it was incorrect, what did you learn from the experiment? What new hypothesis can you create and test? Something is always learned while performing an experiment, even if it's how *not* to perform the next experiment.

Building on past science fair projects

Just as scientists advance the work of other scientists, you can advance the work of those who have performed other science fair projects before you. Don't copy their work, but think of what the next logical step might be to take in that line of research. Possibly you can put a new twist on a previous experiment. For example, suppose someone else's experiment established that electromagnetic radiation can damage aquatic plant life. You might find out if it harms the microbes that live among the plants. Or, if the original experiment was performed *in vitro* (in a test tube), you might perform a similar experiment *in vivo* (in nature).

Abstracts of previous science fair projects are available from the Science Service in Washington DC. (This and other sources of successful science fair projects are listed in Appendix B.)

Getting started

Because you are looking through this book, you probably have an interest in the environment. Therefore, the first thing to do is find out specifically what interests you, if you don't already know. There are several ways to do this.

Use this book

The first thing to do is look through the table of contents for topics to research. When you see one that looks interesting, read through its "Background" and "Project overview." Remember that every project in this book can be adjusted, expanded upon, or fine-tuned in some way to personalize your investigation.

After reading through these sections, think about how you can put your own signature on the experimentation. The "Going further" and "Suggested research" sections are designed to help you personalize each project. If you find yourself saying, "I'd like to know more" about something you see, you're well on your way to selecting a science fair project about our environment.

Other sources

At this point, you can begin your project or continue to look for more insight into the problem. Consider branching out by looking through science sections of newspapers such as the "Science" section in Tuesday's *New York Times*. Also, look at magazines such as *Popular Science*, *Discover*, and *Omni*, which cover a broad range of science topics, or *E Magazine*, *Earth Journal*, *Garbage*, and *BioCycle* for specific interdisciplinary environmental topics. Check the *Reader's Guide to Periodical Literature* in your library, which indexes articles in many magazines and gives a brief synopsis of each. Your school text-

books might also be helpful. Check references to other books, usually found at the end of a chapter.

Other sources that can help include educational television shows
such as "NOVA," "National Geographic" specials, and "Nature." Most
of these types of shows are found on public television and cable net-
works. Check your local listings to see what might be showing in the
near future in your area. Also, don't hesitate to use past science fair
projects as a source of interesting topics.

Talk to specialists in the field

Once you have a good idea for a project, consider talking with a professional. For example, if your project involves pesticides, arrange to
meet an agricultural specialist who works for your state or county, a
professor of entomology at a nearby university, and a farmer who
uses pesticides. If your project involves oil spills, speak with a professional who studies the problem, people affected by the problem,
and those who caused the problem. If you are studying recycling,
speak with the people who recycle, those who don't, and scientists
who study the process. Interesting science fair projects don't only involve equipment, chemicals, and cultures, but also what people have
to say about the topic: pro, con, and neutral.

Also, be sure to use any resources that are readily available. If
you live near a sewage treatment plant, landfill, agricultural research
station, large mechanized farm, small organic farm, or other facility
that can contribute to your project, try to use it to your advantage. If
you have a parent or friend who is involved in a business or profes-
sion applicable to your project, try to incorporate it into your research. The most important thing to remember is to select a project
that you are truly enthusiastic about.

Put your signature on the project

All the projects included in this book are good candidates for science
fair projects. What could make these projects outstanding examples
of research is how you put your signature on it. Did you include portions of the "Going further" section, or delve into the "Suggested research" section? Did a teacher, scientist, or businessperson add an
interesting aspect of the research to make it truly unique and your
own?

Before you begin

Before starting your project, review the entire project with your sponsor to anticipate problems that might arise. Some projects must be done at a certain time of year. Some can be done in a day or two, while others can take a few weeks, months, or even longer.

Some projects use supplies that are found around the home, but many require equipment or supplies that must be purchased from a local hardware store, science or nature store, or a scientific supply house. Some projects require organisms such as microbial cultures or insects. Your sponsor might have access to the organisms needed for the project. Organisms such as insects might be caught in the wild, bought at a pet or bait shop, or ordered from a scientific supply house. Bacterial cultures might be available from your school, or they too can be ordered from a supply house.

Each project in this book states not only what organisms and equipment are needed, but also how or where they might be procured. Much of the equipment and supplies, such as collecting nets, petri dishes, magnifying glasses, and microscopes, might be available at your school and need not be procured on your own. Some projects require that you rear or culture organisms and demand considerable attention before you begin the actual research.

Also, plan ahead financially. Look through the "Materials list" of each experiment. Be sure to add materials you need for additions or modifications you make to the original project. Determine how and where you will get everything and how much it will cost. For example, if a dissecting microscope is needed, do you have access to one? If a live insect is needed, can you catch it in your location at this time of year or must it be ordered from a supply house? If you need a bacterial culture, is it available from your teacher, a nearby university, or must you purchase it? How much will it cost? Don't begin a project unless you can budget the appropriate amount of time and money as suggested by your sponsor.

Performing the experiment

Once you have carefully selected a project by following the previous suggestions, use the following suggestions to organize your experiment.

Scheduling

Before proceeding, it is a good idea to develop a schedule to ensure you have a complete project in time for the fair. Leave yourself time to acquire the equipment, supplies, and organisms. Have your sponsor approve your timetable.

Most science fair projects require at least a few months from start to finish if they are to be accomplished thoroughly, although some can (or must) be completed in less time. In any case, it would be difficult to produce a prize-winning project without plenty of time. Here is a chronological list of things to include when preparing a timetable:

- Identify your adult sponsor.
- Choose a general topic.
- Establish a project notebook for all note-taking throughout the project.
- List resources (such as libraries to go to, people to speak with, businesses, organizations, or agencies to contact).
- Select reading materials and use bibliographies for more resources; begin a formal literature search.
- Select the exact project and develop a hypothesis; write a detailed research plan and discuss it with your adult sponsor; have the sponsor sign-off on your final plan.
- Procure equipment, supplies, organisms and all other materials.
- Follow up on your resource list: speak with experts, make all contacts, etc.
- Set up and begin experimentation.
- Collect data and rigorously take notes.
- Begin to plan for your exhibit display.
- Begin writing your report.
- Begin to analyze data and draw conclusions.
- Complete your report and have your sponsor review it.
- Design your exhibit display.
- Write the final report and abstract, and be sure your notebook is available and readable.
- Complete and construct a dry run of the exhibit display.
- Prepare for questions about your project.
- Disassemble and pack your project for transportation to fair.
- When the fair arrives, set up your display and enjoy yourself.

Literature search

As you can see from the suggested schedule, one of the first items is to perform a full-blown literature search of the problem you intend to study. A *literature search* (also often called simply *research*) means reading everything you can get your hands on about the topic. Read newspapers, magazines, books, abstracts, and anything related to the specific topic to be studied. Use online (computer) databases if available. Talk to as many people as possible who have some insight into the topic. Listen to the news on the radio and television. At this point you might want to narrow down or even change the exact problem you want to study.

Once your literature search is complete and you have organized the data both on paper and in your mind, you should know exactly what problem you intend to study and then formulate your hypothesis.

The research plan

At this point you should have completed a research plan. You can use portions of this book to get started with your research plan, but you must go into additional detail and include all modifications. Before beginning the project, go through it in detail with your sponsor to be sure the requirements of the project are safe, attainable, suitable, and practical. In many science fairs, your sponsor is required to sign off on the research plan, attesting to the fact that it has been reviewed and approved.

It is important to review your particular fair regulations and guidelines to be sure your project won't run into any problems as you proceed.

Science fair guidelines

Almost all science fairs have formal guidelines or rules. Check with your sponsor to see what they are. For example, there might be a limit to the amount of money that can be spent on a project or the use of live (vertebrate) animals. Be sure to review these guidelines and check that the experiment poses no conflicts.

Many science fairs require four basic components for all entries:

1 The actual notebook used throughout the project that contains data collection notes. Be sure to consider this when taking your notes, since they might be read by fair officials.
2 An abstract of the project that briefly states the problem, proposed hypothesis, generalized procedures, data collection methods, and conclusions. This is usually no more than 250 words long.
3 A full-length research paper.
4 The exhibition display.

The research paper

A research paper might be required at your fair, but consider doing one even if it isn't necessary. (You might be able to get extra credit for the paper in one of your science classes.) The research paper should include seven sections:

1 A title page.
2 A table of contents.
3 An introduction.
4 A thorough "Procedures" sections.
5 A comprehensive "Discussion" section explaining both what you did and what went through your mind while performing the research and experimentation.
6 A separate "Conclusion" section that summarizes your results.
7 References and credits listing your sources and giving credit to any person, company, organization, or agency that assisted you.

Books listed in the "Further reading" bibliography of this book explain in detail how to write a research report.

The exhibition display

The exhibit display should be as informative as possible. Keep in mind that most people, including the judges, will only spend a short time looking at each presentation. Try to create a display that gets as much information across with the least amount of words, as quickly as possible. Use graphs, charts, and tables to illustrate data. As the old saying goes, "A picture is worth a thousand words." Make your display as attractive as possible; you cannot communicate the value of your project if you don't draw peoples' attention to it.

Discuss with your sponsor any exhibit requirements, such as special equipment, electrical outlets, and wiring needs. Live organisms of any kind are usually prohibited from being displayed. Often, preserved specimens are also prohibited. Usually no foods, wastes, or even water is allowed in an exhibit. Also, flames, gases, or harmful chemicals are usually not allowed. Find out what you can and cannot do before proceeding.

Many fairs have specific size requirements for the actual display and its backboard. (For more information on building an exhibit display, see the bibliography at the end of this book.)

Judging

When beginning your project, remember that adherence to the scientific method and attention to detail is crucial to the success of any project. Judges usually want to see a well thought-out project and a knowledgeable individual who understands all aspects of the project.

Most science fairs assign a point value to various aspects of a project. For example, the research paper might be worth x points while the actual display might be worth y points. Request any information that might give you insight about the judgment criteria at your fair. This can help you allocate your time and resources where they are needed most.

Part 2

Applied ecology

Applied ecology deals with environmental problems as they affect our society directly. Included in this section are projects about the use of bug lights, commonly heard zapping away through the summer months, an investigation about the wax applied to fruits and vegetables we eat, and composting as an alternative to landfills and incinerators.

Other projects in this section study how microbes can be used to clean up oil spills along beaches and how a modeling program on your personal computer can analyze ultraviolet radiation in your hometown, now and in the future.

4

Bug lights

More harm than good?

(Using bug lights efficiently)

The glow of purple lights and their accompanying zapping sounds are common sights and sounds in cities, suburbs, and the country during the hot summer months. These "bug lights," as they are often called, attract insects with an ultraviolet (UV) light and kill them with an electrical grid that surrounds the light.

An insect's visible light spectrum is different than that of humans. People cannot see the UV end of the light spectrum, but insects can. Many night-flying insects appear to be attracted to these wavelengths.

Project overview

Some people leave their bug lights on all night, while others only turn them on when they are outdoors on their porch, patio, or lawn. (See Fig. 4-1.) The primary reason for using these lights is to reduce the number of annoying, biting insects such as mosquitoes. But most insects are not pests. In fact, many are beneficial since they kill the harmful insects. Do bug lights differentiate between "good" and "bad" insects?

We can group insects into three informal categories:

1 Noxious insects that include biting flies such as mosquitoes and gnats.
2 Plant pests that damage gardens or other cultivated crops and include many leafhoppers and weevils.
3 Beneficial insects, including many small parasitic wasps, that help control insect pests.

4-1 *The "zapping" sound of bug lights is common during the summer months in the cities and the country.*

Do bug lights kill members of all three groups? What percentage of each is the catch? If they kill members of all three groups, can beneficial insects be protected by using these lights at certain times of the night? Begin your literature search to find answers to these and any other questions your research leads you to and formulate your hypotheses. This project is best performed during the hot summer months, but can be done from late spring to early fall.

Materials list

- One or two bug lights. (These devices usually have a cylindrical purple bulb surrounded by a metal grid that conducts electricity. They are usually about 1 foot high and about 5 inches in diameter. There is a tray that catches the dead bugs after they are "zapped." Two identical bug lights can cut the duration of this project in half.)

- An automatic outdoor electric timer to turn the light on and off at exact intervals. (If you use two bug lights, you'll need two timers.)
- A box of plastic zip-lock bags to hold dead insects
- A marker to label each bag
- Forceps and a small paintbrush (such as those in model airplane kits) to manipulate the dead insects for identification
- A dissecting microscope or a high-quality hand lens to help identify dead insects
- An insect identification guide

Procedures

First, find a location to be tested. A porch overlooking a lawn, garden, or field would be good, but it could be anywhere you or someone you know routinely uses a bug light. You will turn the bug light on for one-hour intervals, after which the dead insects will be collected and identified. This will be done for each hour interval through out the night and repeated several times.

To begin, prepare the bug light at the site you've selected. Beginning one hour before dusk, turn the bug light on and record the start time. Exactly one hour later, turn off the light, *unplug the device,* and place all the dead insects caught in the tray into a plastic bag. Label the bag with the date, time interval and location. (See Fig. 4-2.)

4-2 *Use ziplock plastic bags, each labeled with the hour interval, to collect the insects that have been "zapped."*

Repeat this process for the next one hour interval, noting the start time. Keep repeating this process hourly until you have had enough for that night. Use the automatic timer to turn the light on and off for another hour interval. You can collect these bugs the next morning.

This procedure must be repeated until collections have been made for each hour interval from before dusk through sunrise in the morning. After completing the first collection series, you must replicate the procedure by making a second collection. (If you have two identical bug lights and two timers, you can double the number of collections made each night.)

As soon as some of the collections have been stored, begin the identification and counting process. (If you are not going to begin identifying the insects within a few days of collection, they should be placed in jars filled with 70% alcohol to preserve them.) Since the insects have been "zapped," they will be damaged, but should be identifiable.

Use forceps to manipulate the insects, a dissecting microscope or hand lens, and an identification guide to categorize the collected insects into one of three groups: noxious (biting), plant pests, or beneficial. To do this, you will usually have to identify them to the "superfamily" level. For example, weevils, which are plant pests, belong to the superfamily *Curculionoidea*; many parasitic wasps, called *Ichneumons*, are beneficial and belong to the superfamily *Ichneumonidea*; and mosquitoes which we all know to be noxious belong to *Culicoidea*, which also includes midges and gnats. Count the numbers of each type, filling in a table similar to Table 4-1 as you identify and count the catch for each hour interval.

Table 4-1

Hour	Insect type	Number	Category (B)eneficial (N)oxious (P)lant pest	Notes
8–9 PM	Mosquito	IHI II	N	
	Plant hopper	I	P	
	Weevil	I	P	
	?	II	?	Could not identify
9–10 PM				

Take the numbers from the second collection series and use the average of both groups for each hour interval. Total all the insects into the three groups (noxious, pests, beneficial) for each hourly interval throughout the night. After all your raw data has been collected, analyze the data.

Analysis

Use the raw data collected to plot a graph of the three types of insects over the course of the night as you see in Fig. 4-3. Do bug lights kill all three types of insects? Draw a pie chart that shows what percentage of the total came from each of the three groups. If they kill all types, are there certain times when individuals from each group are more likely to be killed? Is it possible to turn the light on or off at certain times in order to kill only annoying insects or plant pests, but not harm beneficial insects?

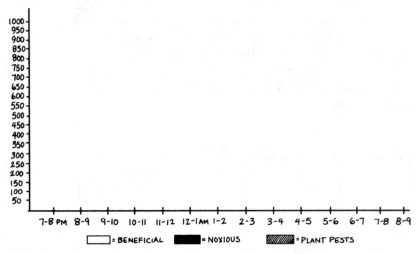

4-3 *Create a graph similar to this one to illustrate the groups of insects collected throughout the night.*

Going further

- Do these bug lights attract more insects into an area than they kill? Would you be attacked by biting insects less often if a bug light were not present? Devise an experiment that would determine whether a bug light actually attracted more insects into an area than were being killed by the light.

- Devise an experiment to see if bug lights work better in some habitats than in others. Is a bug light more useful to city dwellers than to those in the country?

Suggested research

- Study insect vision. Is there any hard scientific evidence that UV light attracts insects better than wavelengths within the visible spectrum?
- Investigate the use of pheromone traps to kill insect pests.

5

Waxed fruit

What you see is not what you get

(Using thin-layer chromatography to study waxed fruit)

Background

You have probably noticed that cucumbers purchased at most super-markets appear to have a thick waxy layer covering the surface. The wax is applied to prevent shriveling and thereby prolong the shelf life of the vegetable. It is also supposed to improve its appearance.

This wax may be embedded with fungicides that are applied after harvest to prevent mold growth and can also seal in pesticide residues that remain on the fruit at harvest. Washing the fruit in water does nothing to remove the wax. Peeling away the skin on fruits and vegetables remove the wax but reduces their nutritional value. Cucumbers are the most noticeably waxed produce, but they are not the only ones. Apples, bell peppers, citrus fruits, eggplants, squash, and tomatoes may be waxed as well.

Few people know that a federal law (issued by the Food and Drug Administration) requires waxed produce to be labelled as such. Stores can be fined $1,000 for failing to post this information. The law is rarely enforced and therefore rarely adhered to. If complaints to the store don't resolve the problem, the violation can be reported to your state attorney general's office.

Project overview

Many people are becoming more aware of the health dangers and environmental problems associated with pesticide use. They are looking for alternatives to the use of pesticides and other artificially introduced substances such as wax. Products that meet these conditions are often considered health foods or placed under the category of organically grown products.

This project studies whether produce has been waxed at all, and if so, how many different types of wax have been applied to each. By getting produce from a variety of stores, you will also see differences in the number of waxes applied to produce sold at each store.

Thin-layer chromatography is used to separate out the waxes found on produce. This process requires materials found in most high school laboratories. The "Going further" and "Suggested research" sections give information on using more sophisticated techniques that might only be available at colleges or universities.

Is wax applied to produce purchased from local supermarkets and organic food stores? If wax is found, how many kinds of waxes are applied on each type of produce? Do all stores sell produce containing the same kinds of wax? Begin your literature search to find answers to these and any other questions your research leads you to, and formulate your hypotheses. This project can be performed at any time of year.

⚠ **Warning!** This project involves the use of dangerous chemicals. It must be performed under the strict supervision of your sponsor. As indicated in the "Procedures" section, most of the steps must be performed under a fume hood.

Materials list

- Access to a fume hood
- Safety goggles, protective gloves, and protective clothing
- A sampling of fruits and vegetables from a local supermarket and a store specializing in organically grown foods
- Bags for storing fruit
- Two silica gel plates (5×20 cm) for thin-layer chromatography
- A glass development chamber. (You can build one using a jar large enough to enclose one of the silica gel plates, standing up. See "Procedures.")

- Four microcapillary tubes
- Bulb pipet
- Forceps
- Several small vials with screw caps (large enough to hold 5 ml of liquid)
- A hand-held UV light
- A fine-mist spray bottle
- Filter paper
- The following chemicals:
  - 500 ml of hexane
  - 20 ml of diethylether
  - 2 ml of formic acid
  - 23.5 ml of 95% methanol
  - 2.5 ml of 2'7'- dichlorofluorescein
  - nitrogen gas (optional)

Procedures

You will purchase produce at a variety of food stores, use a solvent to remove the wax if it exists, and analyze the wax in a development chamber using thin-layer chromatography.

To begin, select two or three kinds of fruits from those mentioned in "Background" that you want to test. (Make one of them cucumbers.) Go to your local supermarket and purchase four of each type of produce you've selected to study. (Smaller fruits and vegetables are preferred since wax removal will be easier.) Next, buy four pieces of the same type of produce from a store that specializes in organically grown produce. Do this for each store to be tested. Keep each group in separate, labelled bags.

⚠ **Warning!** All of the remaining steps must be performed under a fume (ventilation) hood with your sponsor's supervision. (See Fig. 5-1.) Wear protective gloves, goggles, and clothing.

The next step is to remove the waxes from the fruit. Pour 100 ml of hexane into a 300 ml beaker. Using forceps, rinse the first group of four fruits or vegetables in the hexane for one minute to strip the wax off. Be sure to rinse the entire fruit or vegetable.

Now, you want to concentrate the solution. Evaporate all but 1 to 2 ml of the hexane containing the wax (in the beaker) by blowing a stream of nitrogen gas into the beaker while under a fume hood. (If you don't have access to nitrogen gas, simply leave the beaker uncovered within the hood. This, however, will take much longer.) Use a pipette to transfer the remaining solution from the beaker to a

5-1
*You must use a fume
hood while performing
this experiment.*

small, screw-cap vial for storage. Be sure to label each vial. Repeat
this process for each of the groups. For example, if you purchased
four apples and four cucumbers at two stores, you will have 16 vials.

Next you need to create the solvent that will carry the waxes up
the gel plate during thin-layer chromatography. Have your sponsor
create a solution consisting of

- 80 ml of hexane
- 20 ml of diethylether
- 2 ml of formic acid

Once the solvent is ready, you can prepare the development chamber to accommodate the gel plate.

Use a screw-top jar large enough to hold the gel plate as you see in
Fig. 5-2. Line the side of the jar with filter paper as you see in the illustration. Leave enough space above the paper for the top of gel plate to
rest against the glass side of the jar, as in Fig. 5-2A. Also leave a vertical
opening so you can see the gel plate clearly, as in Fig. 5-2B. Next, pour
the solvent created earlier into the jar until it is about 1.5 cm deep, as in
Fig. 5-2C. The filter paper will absorb some of the solvent. After the paper is damp, check that there is still enough solvent left for the bottom
of the gel plate to be immersed as you see in the illustration.

Now that the development chamber is ready, prepare the gel
plate with the wax solutions prepared earlier, currently stored in the
vials. Place a microcapillary tube into the first vial and lightly touch it

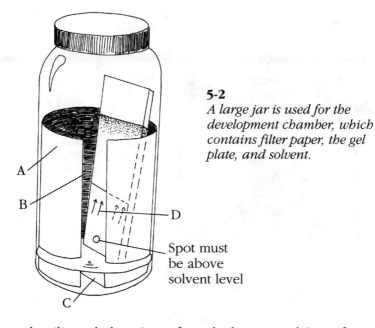

5-2
A large jar is used for the development chamber, which contains filter paper, the gel plate, and solvent.

A

B

D

Spot must be above solvent level

C

to the silica gel plate, 2 mm from the bottom and 5 mm from the left edge. (See Fig. 5-3.) Touch the tube to the plate very briefly—don't hold it to the plate. Don't press too hard or you'll puncture a hole in the gel. As you apply the spot, blow gently on the spot to help keep the spot small.

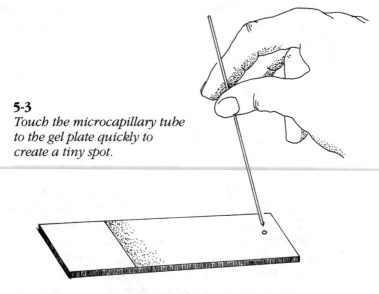

5-3
Touch the microcapillary tube to the gel plate quickly to create a tiny spot.

Spotting the gel plate

Let the spot dry completely and then repeat the process again. Once again, let it dry and repeat. In total you will touch the micro-capillary tube to the same spot three times. The object is to keep the spot small but concentrated. After establishing the first spot at the left edge of the plate, you can place another spot using the same technique at the right hand edge. If you wish, place a third spot in the middle of the plate, but make sure there is at least 5 mm between all spots and from the edge of the plate. All the spots must be 2 mm from the bottom of the plate, as shown in the illustration. Once all the spots on the plate are completely dry, you are ready to place the plate inside the development chamber.

Carefully place the plate into the development chamber so it stands on its end as shown in Fig. 5-2. The bottom should be immersed in the solvent, but the spots must be above the solvent. The edges of the plate should not touch the saturated filter paper either on the top or the sides.

Once all is ready, place the cover back on the chamber. The solvent will rise up the gel plate by capillary action. The gel will become noticeably wet from the solvent, as in Fig. 5-2D. When the solvent has reached within 2 cm of the top of the coated gel surface, remove the plate from the chamber and immediately mark with a pencil where the solvent stopped. This is called the *solvent front*. (See Fig. 5-4.) If you don't do this immediately, the solvent evaporates and the solvent front disappears.

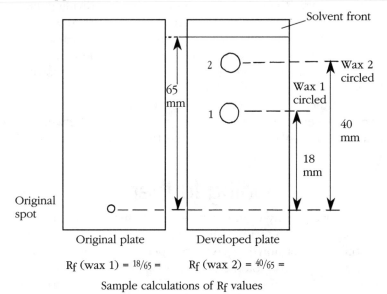

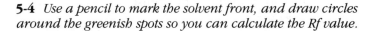

$$R_f \text{ (wax 1)} = {}^{18}\!/_{65} = \qquad R_f \text{ (wax 2)} = {}^{40}\!/_{65} =$$

Sample calculations of R_f values

5-4 *Use a pencil to mark the solvent front, and draw circles around the greenish spots so you can calculate the Rf value.*

The final step is to develop the plate so the wax becomes visible. Prop the plate against a solid surface and allow to dry. Prepare a mixture of 0.1% solution of 2',7'-dichlorofluorescein in 95% methanol. Do this by mixing 2.5 ml of the dichlorofluorescein with 23.5 ml of the methanol. Place this solution into a fine-mist spray bottle. First practice spraying on some cardboard or paper; the trick is to get a uniform coverage. When you are ready, hold the bottle about 6 inches away from the plate and make seven uniform passes over it. Do not overspray the plate.

To view the wax on the plates, bring the plate into a semidark room and place it under a UV light source. You should see a few large, greenish spots that contain the wax from the fruit. Circle them with a pencil so they can be seen without the UV light. Repeat this entire procedure for each of the solutions in the vials.

Analysis

Once you have collected all your data from all the samples, analyze the data first by calculating the *ratio to front* (Rf) value for each. This value helps distinguish between the different substances that were in the samples. Different waxes will have different values. Since different waxes have different affinities for the various substances within the solvent, they travel up the plate at different rates. Some will travel up the plate farther than others. The ratio to front is determined by dividing the total distance the solvent traveled (the solvent front you marked with a line) by how far each substance traveled (the green spots you circled).

To calculate the Rf, measure the distance traveled by the substance (x) and the distance traveled by the solvent front (y) as you see in Fig. 5-4. Then divide x by y. Repeat this for each circle on the plate.

Which fruits or vegetables were coated with wax? How many kinds of wax were found? How did the produce differ between those purchased at a regular supermarket and those from an organic food store?

Going further

- Chromatography is an effective, simple method, but other, more high-tech technology is available. See if you can find someone at a university who can perform a similar analysis using a spectrophotometer or mass spectrophotometer.
- Try various methods of removing the wax from the fruit before performing the chromatography. Does washing in soapy water or scrubbing with a brush remove the wax?

Suggested research

- For more information about waxed fruit, contact
Americans for Safe Foods
1875 Connecticut Avenue N.W., #300
Washington, D.C. 20009
- Research the use of pesticides, especially fungicides, to see
how they might be associated with the waxy layer.
- Investigate why more than one kind of wax would be applied
to a fruit or vegetable. What does it accomplish?

Composting goes high-tech

(Maximizing the efficiency of a compost heap)

Waste disposal is becoming one of the biggest environmental dilemmas we face. In the U.S., 160 million tons of solid waste are produced and disposed of each year. That's *three pounds per person per day.* This waste is disposed of in one of three ways: landfills, incineration, or recycling into new products. Landfills and incineration both have serious environmental problems associated with them.

Recycling offers the least harmful method of resolving, at least in part, our waste disposal dilemma. *Recycling* refers to turning any waste product into another useable product. This might mean using the aluminum from an aluminum can to make another can or turning old computer paper into toilet tissue. You might not think of composting as a form of recycling, but it certainly is. Composting is recycling *au natural.* It uses nature to convert organic matter into another useable product—fertilizer. The organic wastes can include lawn clippings, leaves, food wastes, animal wastes, sewage sludge, or just about any other form of organic matter.

About 30% to 40% of the 160 million annual tons of waste is considered compostable, but only 1% is, at this time, actually composted into fertilizer. For this reason, composting can become an important alternative to incinerators and landfills.

Project overview

Composting has historically been a backyard affair. Environmentally aware individuals have been building small compost heaps for decades, turning their waste (which is free) into their fertilizer (which is ex-

34

pensive to buy). Mowing a lawn provides a simple example of how backyard composting can save a person money and help the environment. Many people mow their lawns and dispose of the clippings. Then, to replace the nutrients lost in the clippings, they go out and buy bags of expensive fertilizer. Placing the clippings, along with other household organic wastes such as leftover food, in a small compost heap creates fertilizer and eliminates the need to purchase it.

Large-scale composting has become a scientific hotbed of research and development due to the waste disposal dilemma. Large-scale composting pilot programs are being performed to see if a substantial portion of our waste can be composted instead of incinerated or placed in landfills. Sludge from city sewage treatment plants and organic wastes diverted from municipal solid wastes have been used in large-scale, high-tech composting facilities.

Maximizing the efficiency of the composting process is worthy of study and can be done both in a backyard compost heap or a city compost facility. This project explains how to build a small-scale compost heap that simulates the interior of an actual compost heap. This will enable you to study various aspects of the compost process.

One important factor is the temperature generated within the inner portion of the heap. How does temperature effect the biodegradation of the organic wastes? Does the degradation cease to occur at a minimum and maximum temperature? Why is temperature so important? What factors inside the compost heap control the temperature? Begin your literature search to answer these questions and any others your research leads you to, and formulate your hypotheses.

This project can be done at any time of year. Be aware that this project could produce odors and attract flies or gnats. Both problems can usually be controlled, as explained later.

The apparatus described in this experiment gives you tremendous flexibility in performing numerous types of compost studies. Although all the materials can be purchased individually, the majority can be purchased as a complete kit from Ward's Scientific Supply (see appendix C). This will allow you to concentrate on the experiment instead of the apparatus.

Materials list

- Three plastic or glass bins such as small terraria or aquarium tanks. (Plastic bins with covers often sold in pet stores to hold small reptiles or amphibians are perfect. They are roughly 9×6×6 inches.)

- Thin sheets of a flexible insulating material, enough to wrap the three bins
- Three aerator pumps such as those used to aerate an aquarium. (The smallest, least expensive ones are fine. You might be able to use fewer pumps by using splitter lines so one pump aerates multiple bins.)
- Three 250 ml Erlenmeyer flasks (one for each bin)
- Flexible air line tubing to connect the pumps to flasks and finally to the bin. (This can be purchased at a pet store.)
- Three two-hole rubber stoppers to fit the flasks
- Three 6-inch lengths of glass tubing to extend into the flasks
- A bubble wand kit to aerate the bins. (This consists of a porous tube with the air line attached to one end. The other end is closed off so air bubbles go out through the length of the porous tube. The wand can be purchased from a pet shop.)
- A carbon source such as shredded paper and wood shavings to act as organic matter to be composted
- A source of microbes to get the compost process started and to simulate microbes found in nature. (This should be purchased from a supply house. Don't use compost starter kits available at garden centers; they might contain organisms inappropriate for use in the laboratory.)
- A source of nitrogen to get the compost process going. (This usually includes dried blood and bone meal. This can be purchased from a supply house or an organic gardening center.)
- At least one, and preferably three, thermometers to measure the inner temperature of each bin
- Three hot plates. (Only one or two are needed if they are large plates.)
- Plastic or rubber gloves
- A dissecting microscope
- Soil-moisture testing kit
- A ruler
- A trowel
- Large forceps or garden gloves

Procedures

The project consists of three parts. In the first, you set up three bins to simulate the inner core of a compost heap. The second part monitors the temperature of each bin and shows you how to maintain constant temperatures in each. During this part, you determine what factors affect the temperature within the bins. In the third part, you analyze the end product of each bin for the degree of biodegradation. In the "Going further" section, you can then survey the microbe populations present in each.

Begin by looking at Fig. 6-1 to see the apparatus. All three bins are similar. Hook up the pump to the plastic tubing and the plastic tubing to the rubber stopper. The tubing must go through the stopper and reach to almost the bottom of the flask. (You can use a glass tube on the inside of the stopper if you prefer.) Insert plastic tubing about 1 inch into the other hole in the stopper. Connect this tube to the wand assembly, which will lay flat at the bottom of the bin. The flasks will be placed on a hot plate alongside the bins. (To save on supplies,

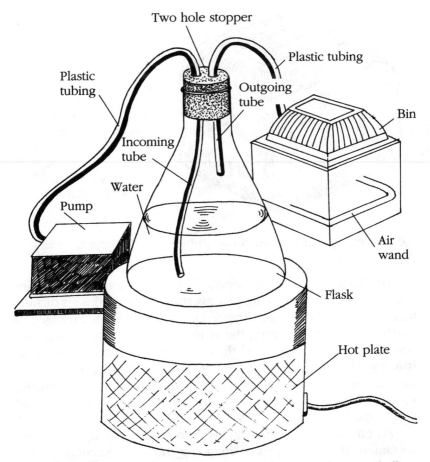

6-1 *This apparatus simulates the interior of a compost heap and allows you to control factors such as temperature and moisture.*

you might be able to have two flasks on one hot plate if it is large enough. If you have a powerful pump, you might be able to use it for two or more bins. Purchase a splitter junction from a pet store that allows one line in, from the pump, and splits the flow to two or three lines out the other side, to the flasks.)

The next step is to prepare the bins. Wrap the insulation around the outside of the bins and tape it in place as shown in Fig. 6-2. Also cut out a piece of insulation to attach to the cover of each bin. Now, prepare the compostable material (the carbon source) by adding two parts of wood shavings to three parts of shredded paper. Mix together and fill each bin almost to the top. Weigh the amount of compostable material prior to placing in the bin. Use the same amounts of each for all three bins.

6-2
The bins should be wrapped in a flexible insulating material.

⚠️ **Warning!** For the remaining portion of this project, wear rubber gloves.

The bins now need an inoculum of microbes and a nitrogen source to get the composting process started. Follow the instructions that came with the nitrogen source and microbe starter package you purchased. If you are using the nitrogen and microbe source from Ward's, you'll add 50 grams of the nitrogen source and follow the instructions for the microbe inoculum. While wearing gloves, mix all the ingredients within the bin. Finally, moisten the contents slightly so they are damp but not dripping wet. Repeat this procedure for all three bins.

Fill one of the flasks halfway with water and hook up the stopper containing the incoming and outgoing tubes as described earlier. Place the flask on the hot plate and turn it on.

⚠️ **Warning!** Since these hot plates will be left on for many weeks, be sure there is no fire hazard. Get approval from your sponsor about the safety of the setup.

Try to maintain a water temperature of 30°C. Be sure the incoming tube goes into the water and the outgoing tube is well above the water line as you see in Fig. 6-1. Repeat this entire procedure for all the bins.

At this point, begin making observations, taking notes, and filling in Table 6-1. Use a thermometer and ruler to read the temperature in the inner core of each bin. Document the temperature and the depth at which the reading was taken. Remain consistent throughout all readings in all bins. Then use a ruler to measure the depth of the bin contents. If you have a soil-moisture test kit, take moisture readings each day, as well. Continue to monitor the core temperature, moisture content, and compost depth every day for all bins. Carefully turn the compost over every day using a trowel. When the temperature reading of all three bins has stabilized as close to 30°C as possible (and the moisture readings are also stable), you are ready to move on to the next part of the experiment.

Table 6-1

LOG SHEET FOR BIN # 1								
Day #	1	2	3	4	5	6	7	8
Core temperature								
Compost depth								
Moisture content								
Turned (#)								

Label one bin "Control," another "Hot," and the last "Cool." (See Fig. 6-3.) You will attempt to maintain the control at 30°C, the hot bin at 30° to 50°C, and the cool bin at 10° to 30°C. This will allow you to determine how temperature affects the biodegradation of organic matter.

Continue the control bin as-is. To raise the temperature for the hot bin, keep the compost wetter than the control and place a layer of insulation directly on top of the compost (under the cover instead of over the cover). Also mix the compost every two or three days instead of once a day. To lower the temperature in the cool bin, keep the compost drier than the control and remove all the insulation from

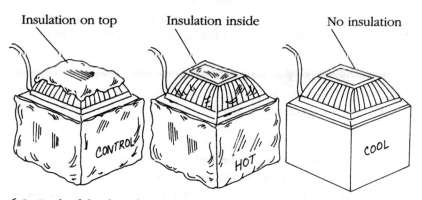

Insulation on top   Insulation inside   No insulation

CONTROL   HOT   COOL

6-3 *Each of the three bins is maintained at different temperatures to see the effect on decomposition.*

around the bin. Also, mix the compost twice each day. Following these procedures, continue to observe the core temperatures, moisture content, and compost depths every day for all bins and document your findings.

While attempting to maintain the proper temperatures, consider manipulating other factors. The amount of insulation can be changed. The insulation helps make the bin simulate the inside core of a compost heap. The ratio of carbon source to nitrogen source, which acts as a food source for the microbes, can be adjusted by adding more of one or the other. The amount of moisture present can be adjusted with a fine-spray water bottle. The number of microbes present at the beginning can be adjusted by adding more starter. The amount of oxygen available for aerobic respiration can be increased or decreased by adjusting the number of times you turn over the heap.

Continue making adjustments until you have stabilized the three bins at the three proper temperature ranges. Continue your observations for about one month. Take detailed notes about how you adjusted the temperature within each bin, since this is a vital part of your experiment.

If flying insects begin to appear around the bins, place a bowl of vinegar near the bins to attract and trap them. If the bins begin to smell from ammonia, they are probably too moist, causing excessive anaerobic activity. Increase aeration by turning more frequently or add more carbon and nitrogen sources to soak up the excess moisture.

At the conclusion of the experiment, take your final temperature, depth, and moisture readings. Using large forceps or garden gloves, remove the material from each bin and carefully observe the physical characteristics of each for degradation. Look at the contents of each bin with a dissecting scope for more detailed observations. Document your findings.

Analysis

What factors did you have to manipulate to adjust the temperature within the bins? Which factors were the most important: moisture content, amount of aeration, or turnover? How do these factors affect the temperature of the bins and why? What is actually generating the heat? What role does aerobic verses anaerobic activity play in this process? Which bin lost the most volume and resulted in the most degraded material and why?

Once you have analyzed your experimental data, consider how what you have learned could be applied to a real compost heap. For example, how much moisture should be allowed into a compost heap, what types of organic matter and at what mixture ratio (carbon to nitrogen) should they be added to the heap, or how often should the heap be turned?

Going further

- At the conclusion of this project, observe the microbial activity in each bin and look for differences in numbers and in diversity of organisms, if any. This can be done by inserting a microscope slide in the bin overnight, fixing the slide with heat, staining, and observing under oil immersion. It could also be done by placing a sample on an agar plate, culturing the inoculation, and then observing.
- Perform a similar experiment, but use three different carbon sources in each bin and maintain the same temperature in each. This will determine which material is the most compostable. After the first part is complete, use the compost from each bin as potting soil to determine which is the best fertilizer.

Suggested research

- Investigate the microflora and microfauna that commonly inhabit a compost heap. What kinds of organisms exist and what are the tolerance ranges for some of the factors studied in the project, such as temperature and moisture?
- Research pilot programs that have been performed on large-scale composting facilities using sludge or municipal solid wastes.

Cleaning up oil spills

Bioremediation

(Using bacteria to clean up oil spills on beaches)

Industrialized nations are literally driven by oil. The world economy is dependent on oil and the world environment is constantly assaulted by its excessive use. Exploration, drilling, refining, transporting, burning, and disposing all take their toll on our planet. Although oil spills are not the most severe attack caused by oil on the planet, they are usually the most visible and dramatic.

When million-gallon spills such as those from the Amoco Cadiz off the coast of Normandy, France occur, and when entire habitats are covered in oil such as that caused by the Exxon Valdez off the coast of Alaska, it makes front page news. Although these are high-profile spills, they are not the primary problem associated with oil spills.

Oil is spilled during normal shipping operations to the tune of five to 10 million tons each year. This oil is released when seawater is used to fill the ship's hold for ballast and then released. Oil spillage also occurs from exploration losses and the normal losses that occur during loading and unloading of ships in port.

These vast volumes of oil have an impact on both local and distant ecosystems. The immediate impact is well-documented and irrefutable. The long-term effects are harder to ascertain, but much of the evidence points to a long-term, detrimental impact to most ecosystems.

The best way to remedy this problem is to minimize the amount of oil spill pollution from the source. Short-term, immediate remedies are also needed to clean up oil spills as soon as they happen. Many methods are currently used, including physical containment such as barriers and skimmers, and chemical substances such as detergents and solvents to help break up the oil. One of the most promising methods is bioremediation—the use of organisms to remove pollutants.

Project overview

When human intervention causes pollution, nature begins a slow and arduous attempt to clean up the mess. Natural processes such as wind, rain, and waves gradually dilute and disperse many pollutants. In some cases, organisms that naturally feed on the pollutant experience a population explosion and help decompose the pollutants, rendering them harmless. Plants are being used to clean up pollutants, including radioactive materials and heavy metals from the soil.

Some organisms actually like to eat oil and oil-based products. These *petrophiles*, as they are called, include some bacteria, yeasts, and fungi. These organisms feed on the oil and break it down as it is assimilated into their bodies. Large numbers of these organisms can help eliminate vast quantities of oil lost during a spill. As these petrophiles produce waste, die, and decompose, they become available to other organisms through food chains. In effect, these organisms help soak up the localized oil spill, convert it into living matter, and distribute it throughout the local ecosystem as food.

Is it practical and feasible to use petrophiles for the bioremediation of the oil spills in real-life situations such as on a beach or a rocky shore? Begin your literature search to answer these questions and any others your research may lead you to, and formulate your hypotheses. This project can be performed at any time of year.

Materials list

- An active culture of *Pseudomonas,* a bacteria (only strains shown to be effective for bioremediation)
- An active culture of *Penicillium,* a fungus. (See appendix B for places to get both cultures. Speak with your sponsor about how to procure and handle these cultures.)
- Special nutrient fertilizer used when the petrophile is released. (See appendix B.)
- Two large test tubes

- Two test tubes with screw caps
- Test tube rack
- Two petri dishes
- Distilled water
- Refined oil
- Fine sand
- Density indicator strips to compare the amount of oil present. (These strips can be created, or see appendix B.)
- Gloves and goggles

Procedures

There are two parts to this project. The first part compares the oil-degrading capabilities of the bacteria and the fungus. The second part determines the feasibility of using these organisms to clean up a beach oil spill and determine which organisms might work better. (Gloves and goggles should be worn whenever handling cultures to prevent contamination.)

Prior to beginning this project, the Pseudomonas and Penicillium cultures must be established and ready for use. Speak with your sponsor about how he or she recommends establishing these cultures. Once the cultures are ready, you can continue with the experiment.

In the first part of the project, you determine the physical characteristics of oil degradation by these two microbes and show how they compare with one another in this process. Label two test tubes with screw caps, one "bacteria" and the other "fungi." Add 5 ml of distilled water to each. Use an eye dropper to add enough refined oil to the test tube to form a thin layer on the top. (This should be about five drops.) Begin your observations by filling in a table similar to Table 7-1. Note the appearance of the oil before inoculation with the microbes.

Inoculate the tube labelled "bacteria" using a sterile pipette to transfer 0.5 ml of the bacterial culture. Repeat this procedure with the tube labelled "fungi." Place the caps on each tube and invert each a few times to mix the water, oil, oxygen and microbes. (See Fig. 7-1.) Incubate the tubes at 30°C, or leave in a warm part of the room. Each day, invert each tube two or three times. Make observations every day for five days. Note the overall appearance, color and turbidity (as explained below) at the surface where the oil and water mix.

The *turbidity*, which is the degree of cloudiness, is an important indicator of the culture growth. The greater the turbidity, the larger the microbe population. There are many methods of reading turbidity levels. Although there are more accurate methods, a simple and relatively accurate technique is the use of density indicator strips. Fol-

Table 7-1

COMPARATIVE RESULTS IN TEST TUBES						
	General Appearance		Color of Oil		Turbidity	
	Bacteria	Fungi	Bacteria	Fungi	Bacteria	Fungi
Day 0						
Day 1						
Day 2						
Day 3						
Day 4						
Day 5						

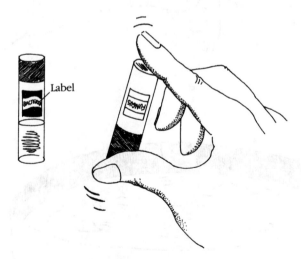

Label

7-1 *Invert the test tubes to mix the solution of water, oil, oxygen, and microbes.*

low the instructions that come with the indicator strips. Note all of your observations in the proper tables.

Now that you see how these microbes degrade oil within the test tube, begin the second part to determine if this process can be applied to a real-life situation such as an oil spill on a beach. Label one petri dish "bacteria" and the other "fungi." Fill both dishes with a level layer of fine sand about 5 mm thick. Add enough distilled water to each dish so the sand is just covered with water. Measure out the amount of water so an equal amount is used in both dishes. The petri dish now simulates a typical beach or sandy shore. Now, add about 20 drops of refined oil over the surface to form a thin layer, which simulates an oil spill. (See Fig. 7-2.) Document your observations of the appearance of the "oil spill" in Table 7-2 before proceeding with the bioremediation process.

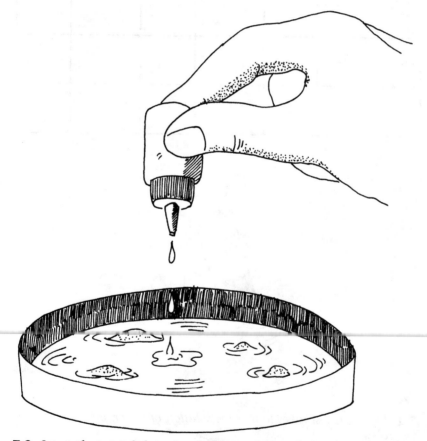

7-2 *Set up the petri dish to simulate a sandy beach damaged by an oil spill.*

Table 7-2

	COMPARATIVE RESULTS ON SIMULATED SANDY BEACH					
	General Appearance		Color of Oil		Turbidity	
	Bacteria	Fungi	Bacteria	Fungi	Bacteria	Fungi
Day 0						
Day 1						
Day 2						
Day 3						
Day 4						
Day 5						

Nutrient fertilizers are often used during microbe bioremediation to act as dispersant and, more importantly, as a food source to help the microbes establish themselves. To simulate this aspect, sprinkle the nutrient fertilizer over the entire layer of oil. Using a sterile pipette, inoculate each petri dish with 1.25 ml of the appropriate culture. Apply the culture throughout the dish. Close the petri dishes and incubate at 30°C or in a warm part of the room.

Make observations every day for five days. Notice the overall appearance of the oil, the color, and the texture. Take readings of the turbidity levels of each and document your observations.

Analysis

For the first part, how did each culture change over time in overall characteristics, color, and turbidity? How did the cultures compare with each other? Were there differences in the final product or in the duration of the degradation? Did they both appear to degrade the oil and show promise as bioremediators?

What happened in the second part of the project to your "beach?" Did one microbe do a better job than the other in cleaning up the spill? What was the result of this bioremediation attempt? What happened to the microbe population at the end of the project and why did it happen? Is either or both of the microbes tested suited for bioremediation of a real beach oil spill?

Going further

- Use the same setup as used in part two of this project, but test whether the nutrient fertilizer actually does anything.
- Use the same experiment, but test for other types of microbial bioremediation.
- Perform a similar experiment, but simulate an oil spill on a rocky shore or some other type of habitat.
- Perform a similar experiment, but test how wave action has an impact on the results or how temperature or some other factor affects the outcome of the oil degradation.

Suggested research

- Investigate other forms of bioremediation, both those in the research and development stages and those in actual use.
- Research other methods of oil spill remediation, such as mechanical and chemical. Find any long-term comparisons of immediate success (the cleanup) and long term success (ecosystem rebound) between these various kinds of remediation.

Computer modeling & the hole in the ozone layer

(Using computer modeling software to analyze UV exposure)

The sun continuously pours ultraviolet (UV) radiation down on our planet. This form of radiation is destructive to most forms of life. It disrupts DNA, causing genetic defects in plants and animals. It can cause eye cataracts and reduces crop yields of corn and rice. Increased levels of UV radiation have been linked to an increased incidence of skin cancer.

We are protected from most of these harmful UV rays thanks to ozone gas that forms a protective layer in our planet's stratosphere. The molecules in this gas consist of three oxygen atoms. When struck with UV radiation, the molecule breaks into smaller pieces, absorbing the harmful energy. Since the smaller pieces later recombine back into another molecule of ozone, the cycle perpetuates itself.

We produce substances categorized as ozone-depleting gases such as *CFCs* (chlorofluorocarbons) that destroy the ozone layer. CFCs are used as refrigerants and in aerosols. When released into the air, these chemicals combine with ozone, reducing its ability to absorb UV radiation. As the ozone layer is destroyed, the amount of UV that reaches the earth increases.

CFCs and most other ozone-depleting gases such as halons (used in fire extinguishers) have been or are being eliminated from use, but the ozone layer is continuing to deteriorate. Only after complete elimination of these gases and many years of "catch-up" will the trend reverse itself.

Project overview

It is estimated that for every 1% loss in the ozone layer, there is a 5% increase in the incidence of skin cancers. UV radiation encompasses a range of wavelengths. UV-B radiation, which falls between wavelengths of 280 and 320 nanometers, is considered the primary culprit in causing these health problems. This direct link between skin cancer (as well as other illnesses) and UV-B radiation is causing many people to reconsider their love for the sun.

Data collected from satellites for many years has helped to piece together a history of how UV levels have changed over time throughout the world. Large volumes of this data, stored in computers, can be used to predict future trends. This is called *computer modeling*. Ecological computer modeling usually uses high-speed supercomputers to analyze the existing data and predict how changes might affect the future.

Ecological computer modeling is now accessible to the typical personal computer user. Save The Planet Software sells a program called "UV B-WARE," which uses data collected via satellite over a 13-year period. This program generates reports that calculate an individual's exposure to UV radiation during a one-year period depending upon that person's location and activities. This program can be used to predict the amount of UV exposure into the future and allow people to determine how to reduce their individual exposure.

How much more UV-B radiation are you and your classmates receiving (at your location) now, compared with 10 years ago, due to ozone depletion? How much more of this radiation will you be receiving 10 years from now due to continued ozone depletion? What lifestyle changes could you and your classmates make over the next ten years to compensate for future increases in UV radiation to keep the levels where they are now? Begin your literature search about these and any other questions your research leads you to, and formulate your hypotheses. This project can be performed at any time of year.

Materials list

- UV B-WARE software available from
  Save the Planet Software
  P.O. Box 45
  Pitkin, CO 81241
  (303) 641-5035
- An IBM-compatible personal computer with hard disk
- A personal analysis of the hours of the day you routinely
  spend indoors and the hours outdoors throughout the year

Procedures

Once you have received the software package, load the program according to the instructions. This project consists of two parts. In the first, you study sample data that comes with the software. This involves using the data about Sam Schoolboy from Chicago. You'll determine how much UV-B radiation Sam is receiving at present, how much less he received 10 YEARS ago, and the percentage of increase expected 10 years into the future.

You'll then edit the sample data to see how Sam can change his lifestyle over the next 10 years to keep the amount of UV-B exposure at its present levels. After a run-through with Sam's data, enter your own data, including your specific location and how much time you spend indoors and outdoors on weekdays and weekends, and create reports.

To begin the project, load the software and spend some time getting acquainted with it. Once you feel comfortable, begin by selecting Calculate Personal UVB Dosages from the main menu. Then, select Next from the menu at the bottom of the screen until Sam Schoolboy appears in the Name field. To view Sam's pre-entered data, select + Window from the menu. Notice how Sam spent each of his weeks during the present year and how much UV-B radiation he was exposed to.

After you've looked over the weekly data, print out the annual report by returning to the main menu and selecting Annual Dosage Report. Select Sam's data and print out the report following the instructions on the screen. Notice the weekly and yearly total UV-B exposure at the bottom of the report. (See Fig. 8-1.)

How much less UV-B exposure would Sam have received 10 years earlier due to a more intact ozone layer? To determine this, re-

```
UV B-Ware  (tm)   Ver. 1.0                      UV DOSAGE ESTIMATE SUMMARY
Name:Sam Schoolboy (sample)   Occupation:Student - age 8   Dosage Year:(1983)
                    Work/Rec  Work Sched.   Rec. Sched.
Week    Location    Days 6..9..N..3...7 6..9..N..3...7   Comments    UVB Dose
  1  177 Chicago     5 2 iioiiiiiiiooii iiooooooooooii typical week    1.06
  2  177 Chicago     5 2 iioiiiiiiiooii iiooooooooooii typical week    1.14
  3  177 Chicago     5 2 iioiiiiiiiooii iiooooooooooii typical week    1.20
  4  177 Chicago     5 2 iioiiiiiiiooii iiooooooooooii typical week    1.36
  5  177 Chicago     5 2 iioiiiiiiiooii iiooooooooooii typical week    1.52*
  6  177 Chicago     5 2 iioiiiiiiiooii iiooooooooooii typical week    1.77*
  7  177 Chicago     5 2 iioiiiiiiiooii iiooooooooooii typical week    2.15*
  8  177 Chicago     5 2 iioiiiiiiiooii iiooooooooooii typical week    2.52*
  9  177 Chicago     5 2 iioiiiiiiiooii iiooooooooooii typical week    2.80*
 10  177 Chicago     5 2 iioiiiiiiiooii iiooooooooooii typical week    3.30*
 11  177 Chicago     5 2 iioiiiiiiiooii iiooooooooooii typical week    3.89
 12  177 Chicago     5 2 iioiiiiiiiooii iiooooooooooii typical week    4.49
 13  177 Chicago     5 2 iioiiiiiiiooii iiooooooooooii typical week    5.13*
 14  125 Orlando     0 7 iiiiiiiiiiiiii iiiooiioooooo1 Disneyworld    20.97
 15  177 Chicago     5 2 iioiiiiiiioooi iiooooooooooo1 typical week    6.67*
 16  177 Chicago     5 2 iioiiiiiiioooi iiooooooooooo1 typical week    7.34*
 17  177 Chicago     5 2 iioiiiiiiioooi iiooooooooooo1 typical week    8.06*
 18  177 Chicago     5 2 iioiiiiiiioooi iiooooooooooo1 typical week    8.67*
 19  177 Chicago     5 2 iioiiiiiiioooi iiooooooooooo1 typical week    9.64*
 20  177 Chicago     5 2 iioiiiiiiioooi iiooooooooooo1 typical week   10.15*
 21  177 Chicago     5 2 iioiiiiiiioooi iiooooooooooo1 typical week   10.85*
 22  177 Chicago     0 7 iiiiiiiiiiiiii iiooooooooooo1 Summer vac.    29.34*
 23  177 Chicago     0 7 iiiiiiiiiiiiii iiooooooooooo1 Summer vac.    31.44*
 24  177 Chicago     0 7 iiiiiiiiiiiiii iiooooooooooo1 Summer vac.    31.81*
 25  177 Chicago     0 7 iiiiiiiiiiiiii iiooooooooooo1 Summer vac.    32.15*
 26  177 Chicago     0 7 iiiiiiiiiiiiii iiooooooooooo1 Summer vac.    32.09*
 27  177 Chicago     0 7 iiiiiiiiiiiiii iiooooooooooo1 Summer vac.    32.97
 28  533 Yellowstone Nat 1 6 iiiiiiiiiiiiii iiooooooooooo1 Summer vac. 28.09
 29  177 Chicago     0 7 iiiiiiiiiiiiii iiooooooooooo1 Summer vac.    32.04*
 30  177 Chicago     0 7 iiiiiiiiiiiiii iiooooooooooo1 Summer vac.    31.06*
 31  177 Chicago     0 7 iiiiiiiiiiiiii iiooooooooooo1 Summer vac.    29.93
 32  177 Chicago     0 7 iiiiiiiiiiiiii iiooooooooooo1 Summer vac.    28.50
 33  177 Chicago     0 7 iiiiiiiiiiiiii iiooooooooooo1 Summer vac.    27.91
 34  177 Chicago     0 7 iiiiiiiiiiiiii iiooooooooooo1 Summer vac.    26.04
 35  177 Chicago     5 2 iioiiiiiiiiooii iiiooooooooooii Back to school 8.39*
 36  177 Chicago     5 2 iioiiiiiiiiooii iiiooooooooooii Back to school 7.57*
 37  177 Chicago     5 2 iioiiiiiiiiooii iiiooooooooooii Back to school 6.92
 38  177 Chicago     5 2 iioiiiiiiiiooii iiiooooooooooii Back to school 6.11
 39  177 Chicago     5 2 iioiiiiiiiiooii iiiooooooooooii Back to school 5.35*
 40  177 Chicago     5 2 iioiiiiiiiiooii iiiooooooooooii Back to school 4.63*
 41  177 Chicago     5 2 iioiiiiiiiiooii iiiooooooooooii Back to school 4.11*
 42  177 Chicago     5 2 iioiiiiiiiiooii iiiooooooooooii Back to school 3.52*
 43  177 Chicago     5 2 iioiiiiiiiiooii iiiooooooooooii Back to school 2.99*
 44  177 Chicago     5 2 iioiiiiiiiiooii iiiooooooooooii Back to school 2.34*
 45  177 Chicago     5 2 iioiiiiiiiiooii iiiooooooooooii Back to school 1.96
 46  177 Chicago     5 2 iioiiiiiiiiooii iiiooooooooooii Back to school 1.69
 47  177 Chicago     5 2 iioiiiiiiiiooii iiiooooooooooii Back to school 1.43*
 48  177 Chicago     5 2 iioiiiiiiiiooii iiiooooooooooii Back to school 1.28*
 49  177 Chicago     5 2 iioiiiiiiiiooii iiiooooooooooii Back to school 1.15*
 50  177 Chicago     5 2 iioiiiiiiiiooii iiiooooooooooii Back to school 1.09*
 51  177 Chicago     5 2 iioiiiiiiiiooii iiiooooooooooii Back to school 1.03
 52  177 Chicago     5 2 iioiiiiiiiiooii iiiooooooooooii Back to school 1.03
                       Total UVB Dose--- (KJoules/sq.meter) ---->   570.64
 * A week/location where UV is stronger than 1980 level, due to ozone loss --> *
```

Weekly dose

8-1 *This is Sam's annual dosage report for 1993. Notice the total UV-B exposure.*

turn to the main menu once again and select Calculate Personal UVB Dosages. Select Sam as you did before, followed by Edit. Press the Enter key until you are in the Dosage Year field. Change the year to be 10 years earlier and press the F10 key to accept this change. To see how much less UV-B radiation Sam would have received 10 years ago, assuming he lived the same lifestyle, return to the main menu by selecting Quit. Select Annual Dosage Report once again and print out this report. What is the total UV-B dosage for that year? (See Fig. 8-2.) How does it compare with the first report?

```
UV B-Ware  (tm)   Ver. 1.0                    UV DOSAGE ESTIMATE SUMMARY
Name:Sam Schoolboy  (sample)     Occupation:Student - age 8    Dosage Year: 1993
                    Work/Rec   Work Sched.   Rec. Sched.
Week   Location    Days 6..9..N..3...7  6..9..N..3...7   Comments     UVB Dose
  1  177 Chicago     5 2 iioiiiiiiiiooii iiooooooooooii typical week    1.18*
  2  177 Chicago     5 2 iioiiiiiiiiooii iiooooooooooii typical week    1.27*
  3  177 Chicago     5 2 iioiiiiiiiiooii iiooooooooooii typical week    1.22
  4  177 Chicago     5 2 iioiiiiiiiiooii iiooooooooooii typical week    1.38
  5  177 Chicago     5 2 iioiiiiiiiiooii iiooooooooooii typical week    1.91*
  6  177 Chicago     5 2 iioiiiiiiiiooii iiooooooooooii typical week    2.24*
  7  177 Chicago     5 2 iioiiiiiiiiooii iiooooooooooii typical week    2.28*
  8  177 Chicago     5 2 iioiiiiiiiiooii iiooooooooooii typical week    2.67*
  9  177 Chicago     5 2 iioiiiiiiiiooii iiooooooooooii typical week    3.26*
 10  177 Chicago     5 2 iioiiiiiiiiooii iiooooooooooii typical week    3.85*
 11  177 Chicago     5 2 iioiiiiiiiiooii iiooooooooooii typical week    4.08*
 12  177 Chicago     5 2 iioiiiiiiiiooii iiooooooooooii typical week    4.71*
 13  177 Chicago     5 2 iioiiiiiiiiooii iiooooooooooii typical week    5.47*
 14  125 Orlando     0 7 iiiiiiiiiiiiiii iiiooiiooooooi Disneyworld    20.37
 15  177 Chicago     5 2 iioiiiiiiiioooi iioooooooooooi typical week    6.83*
 16  177 Chicago     5 2 iioiiiiiiiioooi iioooooooooooi typical week    7.51*
 17  177 Chicago     5 2 iioiiiiiiiioooi iioooooooooooi typical week    8.94*
 18  177 Chicago     5 2 iioiiiiiiiioooi iioooooooooooi typical week    9.61*
 19  177 Chicago     5 2 iioiiiiiiiioooi iioooooooooooi typical week   10.29*
 20  177 Chicago     5 2 iioiiiiiiiioooi iioooooooooooi typical week   10.83*
 21  177 Chicago     5 2 iioiiiiiiiioooi iioooooooooooi typical week   11.99*
 22  177 Chicago     0 7 iiiiiiiiiiiiiii iiooooooooooooi Summer vac.    32.31*
 23  177 Chicago     0 7 iiiiiiiiiiiiiii iiooooooooooooi Summer vac.    32.26*
 24  177 Chicago     0 7 iiiiiiiiiiiiiii iiooooooooooooi Summer vac.    32.65*
 25  177 Chicago     0 7 iiiiiiiiiiiiiii iiooooooooooooi Summer vac.    34.01*
 26  177 Chicago     0 7 iiiiiiiiiiiiiii iiooooooooooooi Summer vac.    33.94*
 27  177 Chicago     0 7 iiiiiiiiiiiiiii iiooooooooooooi Summer vac.    33.01
 28  533 Yellowstone Nat 1 6 iiiiiiiiiiiiiii iiooooooooooooi Summer vac.    29.08*
 29  177 Chicago     0 7 iiiiiiiiiiiiiii iiooooooooooooi Summer vac.    32.54*
 30  177 Chicago     0 7 iiiiiiiiiiiiiii iiooooooooooooi Summer vac.    31.54*
 31  177 Chicago     0 7 iiiiiiiiiiiiiii iiooooooooooooi Summer vac.    29.88
 32  177 Chicago     0 7 iiiiiiiiiiiiiii iiooooooooooooi Summer vac.    28.45
 33  177 Chicago     0 7 iiiiiiiiiiiiiii iiooooooooooooi Summer vac.    27.50
 34  177 Chicago     0 7 iiiiiiiiiiiiiii iiooooooooooooi Summer vac.    25.66
 35  177 Chicago     5 2 iioiiiiiiiiooii iiiooooooooooii Back to school  8.55*
 36  177 Chicago     5 2 iioiiiiiiiiooii iiiooooooooooii Back to school  7.72*
 37  177 Chicago     5 2 iioiiiiiiiiooii iiiooooooooooii Back to school  7.04*
 38  177 Chicago     5 2 iioiiiiiiiiooii iiiooooooooooii Back to school  6.22*
 39  177 Chicago     5 2 iioiiiiiiiiooii iiiooooooooooii Back to school  5.25*
 40  177 Chicago     5 2 iioiiiiiiiiooii iiiooooooooooii Back to school  4.54*
 41  177 Chicago     5 2 iioiiiiiiiiooii iiiooooooooooii Back to school  3.95
 42  177 Chicago     5 2 iioiiiiiiiiooii iiiooooooooooii Back to school  3.38
 43  177 Chicago     5 2 iioiiiiiiiiooii iiiooooooooooii Back to school  3.11*
 44  177 Chicago     5 2 iioiiiiiiiiooii iiiooooooooooii Back to school  2.43*
 45  177 Chicago     5 2 iioiiiiiiiiooii iiiooooooooooii Back to school  2.06
 46  177 Chicago     5 2 iioiiiiiiiiooii iiiooooooooooii Back to school  1.78
 47  177 Chicago     5 2 iioiiiiiiiiooii iiiooooooooooii Back to school  1.55*
 48  177 Chicago     5 2 iioiiiiiiiiooii iiiooooooooooii Back to school  1.39*
 49  177 Chicago     5 2 iioiiiiiiiiooii iiiooooooooooii Back to school  1.19*
 50  177 Chicago     5 2 iioiiiiiiiiooii iiiooooooooooii Back to school  1.12*
 51  177 Chicago     5 2 iioiiiiiiiiooii iiiooooooooooii Back to school  1.05*
 52  177 Chicago     5 2 iioiiiiiiiiooii iiiooooooooooii Back to school  1.05*
            Total UVB Dose ---- (KJoules/sq.meter) ---->    588.10
 * A week/location where UV is stronger than 1980 level, due to ozone loss ---> *
```

Weekly dose

8-2 *This is Sam's annual dosage report for 10 years ago, 1983. Notice the total UV exposure.*

How much more UV-B radiation will Sam receive 10 years from now, assuming he maintains the same lifestyle? To get this information, once again return to the main menu and select Calculate Personal UVB Dosages. Again, select Sam and select the Edit command. Press the Enter key until the cursor is in the Dosage Year field (it now reads 10 years into the past) and change it to 10 years into the future. Press the F10 key to accept the change. See how much more UV-B Sam will be zapped with in 10 years by going back to the main menu, selecting Annual Dosage Report, and printing out this report. How

```
UV B-Ware  (tm)  Ver. 1.0                    UV DOSAGE ESTIMATE SUMMARY
Name:Sam Schoolboy (sample)    Occupation:Student - age 8    Dosage Year: (2003)
                  Work/Rec   Work Sched.    Rec. Sched.
Week   Location   Days 6..9..N..3...7 6..9..N..3...7  Comments    UVB Dose
  1  177 Chicago    5 2 iioiiiiiiiiooii iiooooooooooii typical week     1.34*
  2  177 Chicago    5 2 iioiiiiiiiiooii iiooooooooooii typical week     1.44*
  3  177 Chicago    5 2 iioiiiiiiiiooii iiooooooooooii typical week     1.24
  4  177 Chicago    5 2 iioiiiiiiiiooii iiooooooooooii typical week     1.41
  5  177 Chicago    5 2 iioiiiiiiiiooii iiooooooooooii typical week     2.61*
  6  177 Chicago    5 2 iioiiiiiiiiooii iiooooooooooii typical week     3.05*
  7  177 Chicago    5 2 iioiiiiiiiiooii iiooooooooooii typical week     2.43*
  8  177 Chicago    5 2 iioiiiiiiiiooii iiooooooooooii typical week     2.85*
  9  177 Chicago    5 2 iioiiiiiiiiooii iiooooooooooii typical week     3.91*
 10  177 Chicago    5 2 iioiiiiiiiiooii iiooooooooooii typical week     4.62*
 11  177 Chicago    5 2 iioiiiiiiiiooii iiooooooooooii typical week     4.29*
 12  177 Chicago    5 2 iioiiiiiiiiooii iiooooooooooii typical week     4.95*
 13  177 Chicago    5 2 iioiiiiiiiiooii iiooooooooooii typical week     5.85*
 14  125 Orlando    0 7 iiiiiiiiiiiiiii iiiiooiioooooooi Disneyworld    19.80
 15  177 Chicago    5 2 iioiiiiiiiioooi iiooooooooooi typical week      6.99*
 16  177 Chicago    5 2 iioiiiiiiiiooii iiooooooooooi typical week      7.69*
 17  177 Chicago    5 2 iioiiiiiiiiooii iiooooooooooi typical week      9.99*
 18  177 Chicago    5 2 iioiiiiiiiiooii iiooooooooooi typical week     10.74*
 19  177 Chicago    5 2 iioiiiiiiiiooii iiooooooooooi typical week     11.01*
 20  177 Chicago    5 2 iioiiiiiiiioooi iiooooooooooi .typical week    11.59*
 21  177 Chicago    5 2 iioiiiiiiiioooi iiooooooooooi typical week     13.32*
 22  177 Chicago    0 7 iiiiiiiiiiiiiii iiooooooooooi Summer vac.      35.74*
 23  177 Chicago    0 7 iiiiiiiiiiiiiii iiooooooooooi Summer vac.      33.13*
 24  177 Chicago    0 7 iiiiiiiiiiiiiii iiooooooooooi Summer vac.      33.52*
 25  177 Chicago    0 7 iiiiiiiiiiiiiii iiooooooooooi Summer vac.      36.02*
 26  177 Chicago    0 7 iiiiiiiiiiiiiii iiooooooooooi Summer vac.      35.96*
 27  177 Chicago    0 7 iiiiiiiiiiiiiii iiooooooooooi Summer vac.      33.05
 28  533 Yellowstone Nat 1 6 iiiiiiiiiiiiiii iiooooooooooi Summer vac. 30.12*
 29  177 Chicago    0 7 iiiiiiiiiiiiiii iiooooooooooi Summer vac.      33.06*
 30  177 Chicago    0 7 iiiiiiiiiiiiiii iiooooooooooi Summer vac.      32.04*
 31  177 Chicago    0 7 iiiiiiiiiiiiiii iiooooooooooi Summer vac.      29.83
 32  177 Chicago    0 7 iiiiiiiiiiiiiii iiooooooooooi Summer vac.      28.40
 33  177 Chicago    0 7 iiiiiiiiiiiiiii iiooooooooooi Summer vac.      27.10
 34  177 Chicago    0 7 iiiiiiiiiiiiiii iiooooooooooi Summer vac.      25.28
 35  177 Chicago    5 2 iioiiiiiiiiooii iiiooooooooooii Back to school  8.72*
 36  177 Chicago    5 2 iioiiiiiiiiooii iiiooooooooooii Back to school  7.88*
 37  177 Chicago    5 2 iioiiiiiiiiooii iiiooooooooooii Back to school  7.17*
 38  177 Chicago    5 2 iioiiiiiiiiooii iiiooooooooooii Back to school  6.33*
 39  177 Chicago    5 2 iioiiiiiiiiooii iiiooooooooooii Back to school  5.16
 40  177 Chicago    5 2 iioiiiiiiiiooii iiiooooooooooii Back to school  4.46
 41  177 Chicago    5 2 iioiiiiiiiiooii iiiooooooooooii Back to school  3.79
 42  177 Chicago    5 2 iioiiiiiiiiooii iiiooooooooooii Back to school  3.25
 43  177 Chicago    5 2 iioiiiiiiiiooii iiiooooooooooii Back to school  3.24*
 44  177 Chicago    5 2 iioiiiiiiiiooii iiiooooooooooii Back to school  2.54*
 45  177 Chicago    5 2 iioiiiiiiiiooii iiiooooooooooii Back to school  2.16*
 46  177 Chicago    5 2 iioiiiiiiiiooii iiiooooooooooii Back to school  1.87*
 47  177 Chicago    5 2 iioiiiiiiiiooii iiiooooooooooii Back to school  1.70*
 48  177 Chicago    5 2 iioiiiiiiiiooii iiiooooooooooii Back to school  1.52*
 49  177 Chicago    5 2 iioiiiiiiiiooii iiiooooooooooii Back to school  1.23*
 50  177 Chicago    5 2 iioiiiiiiiiooii iiiooooooooooii Back to school  1.16*
 51  177 Chicago    5 2 iioiiiiiiiiooii iiiooooooooooii Back to school  1.08*
 52  177 Chicago    5 2 iioiiiiiiiiooii iiiooooooooooii Back to school  1.08*
              Total UVB Dose ---- (KJoules/sq.meter) ---->  (608.7)
 * A week/location where UV is stronger than 1980 level, due to ozone loss --> *
```

(Weekly dose — vertical label at right)

8-3 *This is Sam's annual dosage report for 10 years into the future, 2003. Notice the projected total UV exposure.*

much is the UV-B dosage expected to increase over the next 10 years? (See Fig. 8-3.)

You should now have three reports for Sam, the present, 10 years into the past, and 10 years into the future. Now see how Sam could change his lifestyle over the next 10 years to keep the UV-B levels where they are today. From the main menu, go back into the Calculate Personal UVB Dosages for Sam. (It will still be set 10 years into the future.) Select + Window to display the weekly records. Then select Edit. This allows you to change the existing data. You must determine what lifestyle changes Sam can make over the next 10 years to keep UV radiation levels from increasing.

What if Sam decided to remain indoors for one hour, mid-day during seven weeks of his summer vacation? Would this reduction in outdoor activity compensate for the increase in UV-B radiation because of ozone depletion? To see if this is the case, press the Enter key until you are on the Recreation Schedule column. Use the Right Arrow key to move the cursor to the *N* (for noon) column. Change the *o* (outdoors) to an *i* (indoors) under *N* (noon hour). Perform this procedure for seven of the weeks identified as Summer Vacation under the Comments column. (After changing each week, you must press F10 to accept the change, the Down Arrow key to move to the next week, and Edit to get into the fields.)

After editing all seven weeks of data, return to the main menu and once again select Annual Dosage Report. Notice the total UV-B dosage with this new lifestyle taken into consideration. (See Fig. 8-4.) Does it bring the dosage levels back to present-day levels? If so, you've determined how Sam can keep his UV-B dosage at their present levels into the next decade. Print out this final report.

Now that you have a good understanding about how this project works, you're ready to generate reports using real data. Create your own personal dosage calculations instead of using Sam the sample. Select Calculate Personal UVB Dosages, followed by Add. Create a new record by entering your specific Location and Dosage Year. (Start with the current year.) Press F10 to accept the new record. Then select + Window to view the weekly data. The fields will all be empty since this is a new record. Select Add to begin entering your personal lifestyle data. (The last field, Weekly UVB Dose, will be calculated automatically based upon your location, dosage year, and lifestyle information.)

After all the data has been entered, run the report to see what your UV-B dosage is at the present. Then follow the same procedure as you did for Sam to run the report for 10 years into the past and 10 years into the future. Once you know how much of an increase to expect over the next 10 years, see what lifestyle changes you could make over this period that would keep the dosage at today's levels. In other words, how can you change your lifestyle to compensate for the depleting ozone layer?

Analysis

How much UV-B radiation are you now receiving each year? Plot the weekly numbers on a graph. How much more UV-B radiation are you receiving today than 10 years ago? How much more will you be re-

```
     UV B-Ware (tm)  Ver. 1.0              UV DOSAGE ESTIMATE SUMMARY
   Name:Sam Schoolboy (sample)   Occupation:Student - age 8   Dosage Year: 2003
                      Work/Rec  Work Sched.   Rec. Sched.
   ---------------------------------------------------------------------------
   Week  Location     Days 6..9..N..3...7  6..9..N..3...7  Comments    UVB Dose
    1   177 Chicago    5 2 iioiiiiiiiooii iiooooooooooii typical week    1.34*
    2   177 Chicago    5 2 iioiiiiiiiooii iiooooooooooii typical week    1.44*
    3   177 Chicago    5 2 iioiiiiiiiooii iiooooooooooii typical week    1.24
    4   177 Chicago    5 2 iioiiiiiiiooii iiooooooooooii typical week    1.41
    5   177 Chicago    5 2 iioiiiiiiiooii iiooooooooooii typical week    2.61*
    6   177 Chicago    5 2 iioiiiiiiiooii iiooooooooooii typical week    3.05*
    7   177 Chicago    5 2 iioiiiiiiiooii iiooooooooooii typical week    2.43*
    8   177 Chicago    5 2 iioiiiiiiiooii iiooooooooooii typical week    2.85*
    9   177 Chicago    5 2 iioiiiiiiiooii iiooooooooooii typical week    3.91*
   10   177 Chicago    5 2 iioiiiiiiiooii iiooooooooooii typical week    4.62*
   11   177 Chicago    5 2 iioiiiiiiiooii iiooooooooooii typical week    4.29*
   12   177 Chicago    5 2 iioiiiiiiiooii iiooooooooooii typical week    4.95*
   13   177 Chicago    5 2 iioiiiiiiiooii iiooooooooooii typical week    5.85*
   14   125 Orlando    0 7 iiiiiiiiiiiii iiiooiiooooooi Disneyworld     19.80
   15   177 Chicago    5 2 iioiiiiiiiooi  iiooooooooooi typical week     6.99*
   16   177 Chicago    5 2 iioiiiiiiiooi  iiooooooooooi typical week     7.69*
   17   177 Chicago    5 2 iioiiiiiiiooi  iiooooooooooi typical week     9.99*
   18   177 Chicago    5 2 iioiiiiiiiooi  iiooooooooooi typical week    10.74*
   19   177 Chicago    5 2 iioiiiiiiiooi  iiooooooooooi typical week    11.01*
   20   177 Chicago    5 2 iioiiiiiiiooi  iiooooooooooi·typical week    11.59*
   21   177 Chicago    5 2 iioiiiiiiiooi  iiooooooooooi typical week    13.32*
   22   177 Chicago    0 7 iiiiiiiiiiiii  iiooooooooooi Summer vac.     30.20*
   23   177 Chicago    0 7 iiiiiiiiiiiii  iiooooooooooi Summer vac.     27.99*
   24   177 Chicago    0 7 iiiiiiiiiiiii  iiooooooooooi Summer vac.     28.35*
   25   177 Chicago    0 7 iiiiiiiiiiiii  iiooooooooooi Summer vac.     30.51*
   26   177 Chicago    0 7 iiiiiiiiiiiii  iiooooooooooi Summer vac.     30.45*
   27   177 Chicago    0 7 iiiiiiiiiiiii  iiooooooooooi Summer vac.     27.96
   28   533 Yellowstone Nat 1 6 iiiiiiiiiiiii iiooooooooooi Summer vac. 25.76*
   29   177 Chicago    0 7 iiiiiiiiiiiii  iiooooiooooooi Summer vac.    33.06*
   30   177 Chicago    0 7 iiiiiiiiiiiii  iiooooooooooi Summer vac.     32.04*
   31   177 Chicago    0 7 iiiiiiiiiiiii  iiooooooooooi Summer vac.     29.83
   32   177 Chicago    0 7 iiiiiiiiiiiii  iiooooooooooi Summer vac.     28.40
   33   177 Chicago    0 7 iiiiiiiiiiiii  iiooooooooooi Summer vac.     27.10
   34   177 Chicago    0 7 iiiiiiiiiiiii  iiooooooooooi Summer vac.     25.28
   35   177 Chicago    5 2 iioiiiiiiiooii iiiooooooooooii Back to school  8.72*
   36   177 Chicago    5 2 iioiiiiiiiooii iiiooooooooooii Back to school  7.88*
   37   177 Chicago    5 2 iioiiiiiiiooii iiiooooooooooii Back to school  7.17*
   38   177 Chicago    5 2 iioiiiiiiiooii iiiooooooooooii Back to school  6.33*
   39   177 Chicago    5 2 iioiiiiiiiooii iiiooooooooooii Back to school  5.16
   40   177 Chicago    5 2 iioiiiiiiiooii iiiooooooooooii Back to school  4.46
   41   177 Chicago    5 2 iioiiiiiiiooii iiiooooooooooii Back to school  3.79
   42   177 Chicago    5 2 iioiiiiiiiooii iiiooooooooooii Back to school  3.25
   43   177 Chicago    5 2 iioiiiiiiiooii iiiooooooooooii Back to school  3.24*
   44   177 Chicago    5 2 iioiiiiiiiooii iiiooooooooooii Back to school  2.54*
   45   177 Chicago    5 2 iioiiiiiiiooii iiiooooooooooii Back to school  2.16*
   46   177 Chicago    5 2 iioiiiiiiiooii iiiooooooooooii Back to school  1.87*
   47   177 Chicago    5 2 iioiiiiiiiooii iiiooooooooooii Back to school  1.70*
   48   177 Chicago    5 2 iioiiiiiiiooii iiiooooooooooii Back to school  1.52*
   49   177 Chicago    5 2 iioiiiiiiiooii iiiooooooooooii Back to school  1.23*
   50   177 Chicago    5 2 iioiiiiiiiooii iiiooooooooooii Back to school  1.16*
   51   177 Chicago    5 2 iioiiiiiiiooii iiiooooooooooii Back to school  1.08*
   52   177 Chicago    5 2 iioiiiiiiiooii iiiooooooooooii Back to school  1.08*
                    Total UVB Dose ---- (KJoules/sq.meter) ---->   572.39
   * A week/location where UV is stronger than 1980 level, due to ozone loss --> *
```

Weekly dose

8-4 *If you changed Sam's lifestyle in 2003, notice how it changes his exposure to UV radiation.*

ceiving in 10 years if your lifestyle remains the same? How can you change your lifestyle to compensate for this additional dosage? How many different ways can you adjust your lifestyle to accomplish this compensation?

Going further

- Instead of using your personal lifestyle, create, distribute, and collect a survey for your classmates that determines your class's "average lifestyle." Perform the project for the class data instead of your personal data.

- Create profiles for other people and compare the results with your own. How do your parents, teachers, or professional skiers fair when it comes to UV radiation exposure and its accompanying risks?

Suggested research

- Study UV radiation and its effects on plant and animal health in depth.
- Study the history of the ozone "hole" problem. How has it been handled since it first became a concern, up until the present? Look at it from an international perspective. How does it compare with the global warming problem? Can the hole in the ozone teach us anything about other environmental problems?

Part 3

Soil ecosystems

Topsoil contains the two basic components of our biosphere: the *abiota*, which include all the nonliving features such as rocks, minerals, and water, and the *biota*, which are all living things. The topsoil is where both components intertwine, passing substances back and forth between the living and the nonliving worlds.

Earthworms play a vital role in this transitional region, and two of the projects in this section study these organisms. The first looks at how earthworms decompose organic matter and the second investigates the impact of human-induced environmental stress on earthworms.

The third project studies an important and often unappreciated process on our planet—nitrogen fixation. This project investigates how acid rain affects this process. The final project looks into how touch, wind, and rain affects plant growth.

Earthworms & humus

(The relationship between earthworms and humus in the soil)

Topsoil can be thought of as a transitional region between the living and the nonliving worlds. Inorganic material within the soil enters the living world when it is absorbed by plants and passed to animals along food chains and complex food webs. Organisms incorporate these minerals and nutrients into their bodies only to have them returned to the soil when the organism dies or produces waste products. The complex organic molecules are broken back down by organisms that live and feed on the decaying carcasses. The cycle continues when these simpler molecules are returned to the soil to be reused once again by another generation of plants.

Partially decomposed plant and animal matter mixed with the earth is called *humus*. This dark-brown material is considered the ideal topsoil for plant growth, since it is rich in nutrients, the correct texture, and absorbs water well. Insects, earthworms, bacteria, and fungi perform most of the work decomposing organic matter, helping break it down into simple molecules to be used once again.

Project overview

As many as half a million earthworms can live in a 2½-acre field of rich soil. This hoard of earthworms can eat through 10 tons of soil a year. If you find rich, fertile soil, it's a good bet that you'll also find earthworms. The more, the better. Earthworms eat their way through soil and in doing so, combine inorganic material with organic, thoroughly mixing the topsoil and producing humus. Their burrowing also *aerates* the soil, improving its ability to absorb air and drain moisture. As worms deposit waste, they produce a crumbly textured soil, perfect for plant growth.

How quickly can earthworms change organic waste products such as grass clippings into humus? How much humus can earthworms create within a week? Does the presence of earthworms produce visible results within this short period of time? Begin your literature search about these and any other questions your research leads you to, and formulate your hypotheses. If you are purchasing the earthworms, this project can be performed at any time of year.

Materials list

- About 75 earthworms (caught or purchased from a bait store, garden center, or supply house)
- Peat moss
- A few cups of different types of organic waste: grass clippings, leaf litter, leftover foods such as old fruits or vegetables, animal manure, etc.
- Small box of cornmeal
- Six plastic or rubber storage tubs with tops (holding roughly 5 quarts, with dimensions about 13 inches long, 8 inches wide, and 5 inches high)
- Small cup or plant pot, approximately 3×3 inches
- Large spoon
- Dissecting microscope
- Humus testing kit. (This can be purchased from a supply house, or your teacher might have the chemicals in your school lab. This project assumes you are using the soil humus kit by LaMotte. See appendix B for ordering information.)

Procedures

Begin by preparing the earthworms' living quarters. Fill each tub about ¾ of the way to the top with peat moss, which is their bedding material. Now you must make room for the organic matter (grass clippings). Press a cup upside down into the peat moss like a cookie cutter, as shown in Fig 9-1. Then, scoop out the peat moss with a large spoon so a hole the size of the cup remains. Make three such holes in each tub, as you see in Fig. 9-2. Fill all three holes with the same type of organic material, such as grass clippings.

Repeat this procedure using the same type of organic matter in a second tub. You'll have two tubs containing a total of six holes for each type of organic matter tested. Label both tubs with the type of

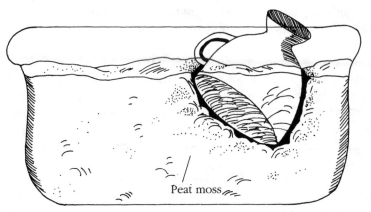

9-1 *Use an upside-down cup like a cookie cutter to make a hole for grass clippings.*

9-2
The hole on the right is being scooped out with a spoon, the one in the middle is already cleared, and the one on the left has already been filled with grass clippings.

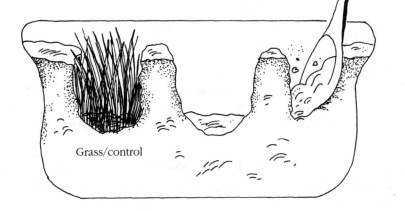

organic matter used, such as "grass." Then label one of the tubs "worms" and the other "control." Repeat this process for the next two tubs using a different kind of organic matter such as leftover food. Then, do two more tubs in a similar fashion for a third type of organic matter.

To make the final preparations for the earthworm abodes, sprinkle about 200 ml of water on the surface of all the tubs. Place 12 healthy earthworms in each of the three tubs labeled "worms." Finally, spread 1 teaspoon of cornmeal over the surface of all the tubs for food. (It will only be used in the tubs with the worms, but it is placed on all the tubs so it is not a variable.) Place the covers over the tubs. Record the date and time and make notes about the physical characteristics of the worms. Keep the tubs out of direct sunlight and away from heat.

Every three days, open the tubs and make observations. Note the physical characteristics of the organic matter. Take a small sample of the organic matter directly from the center of each of the three filled holes and look at it under the dissecting scope to make more detailed observations about its physical condition. Do this for all six tubs. Use a portion of the sample you just removed for use with the humus testing kit to see how much humus is present. Document your data during each observation. (If the material becomes dry, sprinkle additional water on the surface.) Begin filling in Table 9-1.

Continue your observations for three weeks, at which time you can make your final visual observations, take your final humus tests, and make your final detailed observations under the dissecting scope. Carefully observe the physical condition of the organic matter in each tub by using a spoon to dig throughout the area.

Analysis

How did the organic matter appear to the naked eye in each tub? Were there obvious differences between the tubs with worms and those without? Were there any differences in decomposition between the types of organic matter? Was there a substantial difference in the amount of humus created between those tubs with worms and those tubs without? Was three weeks enough time to see a difference in the amount of physical and chemical decomposition between organic matter with and without earthworms?

Going further

- Earthworms are not the only organisms decomposing the soil in these tubs and producing humus. Identify other types of organisms involved in the process by taking a small sample from each tub, placing a drop of water on it, and observing it under a compound microscope. What other organisms are living in these tubs?
- Investigate whether different species of earthworms decompose organic matter more rapidly than others by using a similar experimental set-up.

Table 9-1

GRASS TUB DATA COLLECTION

Tub	Gross Appearance #1	#2	#3	Microscopic Appearance #1	#2	#3	Humus Content #1	#2	#3	Notes
Grass/Worms										
Day 0										
3										
6										
9										
12										
15										
18										
21										
Grass/Control										
Day 0										
3										
6										

Suggested research

- Investigate which of the microscopic organisms that you identified in the first part of "Going further" are actually involved in decomposition and how big a part they play. Will they decompose the soil to the same degree the earthworms did, if given enough time?
- Using earthworms to compost organic wastes has become popular. Earthworm composting kits are available, some even for indoor use. Investigate whether these new products are gimmicks or if they really work.

10

Environmental stress & earthworms

(The effect of substances introduced by humans on the internal anatomy of earthworms)

Background

Topsoil is a microhabitat usually teeming with life. Invisible to the naked eye, complex food webs exist beneath our feet. A single gram of rich soil can contain 2.5 billion bacteria, half a million fungi, 50,000 algae, and 30,000 protozoans. Hundreds of thousands of earthworms can live in an acre of land with countless insects. Earthworms are one of the most important soil organisms, responsible for conditioning the soil and preparing it for plant growth. Rich, fertile soil is usually synonymous with the presence of earthworms.

Whenever we think of environmental damage, we usually think of the impact on large forms of life such as endangered species of mammals or birds. But a much more fundamental effect of environmental stress is how it affects organisms at the lower ends of food chains, such as earthworms. We might not hear about the earthworm being on the endangered species list, but how does environmental stress such as pesticides, fertilizers, and toxic chemical wastes affect the health of these organisms? What are the ramifications to the local ecosystem?

Project overview

Agriculture depends on topsoil for growth. To force as much productivity out of the land as possible, synthetic fertilizers and pesticides are usually used extensively and consistently. When foreign substances are introduced into any ecosystem, there might be an obvious negative impact such as the death of many organisms, or more subtle effects, such as physiological disorders. These disorders can impair the organisms' ability to survive in some way or reduce the reproductive capacity of the individuals.

Studying the effect of a substance such as a pesticide on the anatomy and physiology of organisms is far better than waiting for a species to become endangered or an entire ecosystem to collapse. In the famous case of the pesticide DDT, populations of osprey began to decrease when the byproducts of DDT that had accumulated in the birds prevented females from producing normal eggshells. This fact was not discovered until well after the populations were in decline.

When we apply pesticides and fertilizers to enhance the growth of our plants and crops, are we harming nature's own soil conditioner, the earthworm? Do commonly used pesticides and fertilizers affect the gross anatomy of earthworms? Begin your literature search about these and any other questions your research leads you to, and formulate your hypotheses. This project can be performed at any time of year, as long as you have access to earthworms.

Materials list

- 10 plastic or rubber storage tubs with tops (holding roughly 5 quarts with dimensions about 13 inches long, 8 inches wide, and 5 inches high)
- About 50 earthworms (caught or purchased from a bait store or supply house)
- Peat moss or the same soil where the earthworms were collected, for bedding material
- Small box of cornmeal for earthworm food
- Three different types of pesticides in spray formulations that are available at your local gardening center. (It would be easiest to use those that come in a spray bottle so you won't have to mix the solution. One of the pesticides should be BT, which stands for Bacillus thurengensis. This is a biological control agent pesticide.)
- Fertilizer designed for spraying. (Most need to be mixed with water to produce a liquid formulation.)

- Dissecting pan
- Dissecting scope
- Dissecting kit (simple kit for studying invertebrate anatomy with scissors, scalpel, dissecting pins, forceps, and probes)
- Alcohol
- Distilled water
- Petri dish
- Rubber gloves
- Pipette

Procedures

⚠ **Warning!** Pesticides are dangerous. Follow the instructions on the labels carefully. Discuss these procedures with your sponsor.

You will maintain earthworms in habitats sprayed with various pesticides and a fertilizer for a few weeks. At intervals you will look for changes in the gross external and internal anatomy of the earthworms.

To prepare a home for the worms, fill each of the 10 tubs about half-way to the top with either topsoil or peat moss to act as a bedding material. Place five earthworms in each tub. Since each pesticide or fertilizer will be applied to two tubs and two tubs will be used as controls, label all the tubs appropriately. (See Fig. 10-1.) Place the tops on the tubs and allow the earthworms to get acclimated to their new environment. Keep the tubs out of direct sunlight or any other heat source. Begin your note-taking.

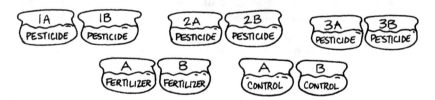

10-1 *There will be five sets of two tubs. Three sets are used for pesticides, one for fertilizer, and one as a control.*

After 24 hours you can continue. Sprinkle 1 teaspoon of cornmeal over the surface of each tub as a food supply. Apply each pesticide to the appropriate two tubs by following the instructions on the can or bottle. (See Fig. 10-2.) Do this outside, not in your home or school lab. Keep the tubs outdoors, but in a protected place. Apply as if you were actually applying to a miniature lawn or garden.

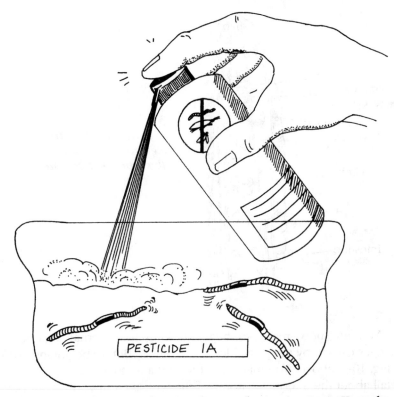

PESTICIDE IA

10-2 *Apply the pesticide according to the instructions. Keep the tubs outdoors.*

Apply the fertilizer to the next two tubs. Once again follow the instructions on the label as if it were actually being applied to a miniature lawn or garden. Use the recommended concentration and application. Leave the last two tubs as-is for the controls. Finally, sprinkle 200 ml of distilled water over the surface of each tub. This simulates rainfall and supplies moisture.

Replace the covers and place the tubs back in a safe place for one week. After that time, begin your observations. Wearing rubber gloves, observe the external anatomy of three earthworms from each tub and take notes. Observe the skin color and texture and the overall condition of each worm. Put them down and notice their movements as well. Observe their heartbeat under the dissecting scope. (You'll need a light source from beneath the stage to do this.) Take notes on each, including the controls, and then place them back into their respective tubs.

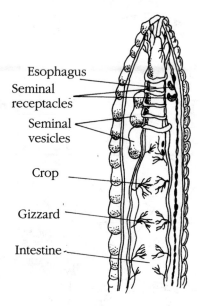

Esophagus
Seminal receptacles
Seminal vesicles

Crop

Gizzard

Intestine

10-3
After dissecting the earthworm, concentrate your observations on the reproductive and digestive systems.

You are now ready to begin looking for internal anatomical changes caused by the pesticides and fertilizer. Before beginning, look at Fig. 10-3, above. You might want to find a textbook that gives more detail about the internal anatomy of the typical earthworm. Your biology text or lab book probably shows the anatomy and has instructions on how to perform an earthworm dissection. If not, find in your library or bookstore William Berman's book *How to Dissect, Exploring with Probe and Scalpel,* published by Prentice-Hall.

First, dissect one of the worms from the control tubs. Place one worm in a petri dish filled with alcohol, which will kill the worm and prepare it for dissection. After a few minutes, place the worm in the dissecting pan and perform an autopsy by following the dissection technique described in the book.

As you proceed, be especially observant of the digestive system and reproductive structures such as the seminal vesicles. Compare what you see with the illustrations. Look at the dissected worm beneath a dissecting microscope. Draw your own illustrations. After completing the autopsy on a worm from the control tub, repeat the dissections and observations on one worm from each of the other tubs. First, do each of the pesticides and then the fertilizer. Look for enlarged, swollen organs in the worms. Keep track of the worms and document your observations.

After all the dissections are complete, sprinkle more food into each tub and repeat the application of each pesticide and the fertilizer to the appropriate tubs. Finally, apply water once again and place the tubs back in a safe place for another week. After that time, repeat the observations and dissections again. This entire procedure can be repeated for a few months or until you feel you have collected sufficient data.

Analysis

Did any of the worms living in habitats sprayed with one of the pesticides or fertilizer show any differences, either externally or internally, when compared with the control worms? Did skin color or texture, behavior, heartbeat, or any anatomical structures appear different than the controls? If so, which substance produced the most change? If the substance was a pesticide, what are the active ingredients and what might the cause of the change have been? If you continued the experiment, did any of the earthworms in any of the groups die? What effect might the results have on the local ecosystem?

Going further

- The easiest way to continue this experiment is to use additional substances as the independent variable. Use other types of pesticides, making sure they all have different active ingredients. Also use substances such as waste water or automotive waste oil.
- Select one substance that has been shown to produce anatomical changes in the reproductive system and rear these worms through to produce young. Compare the offspring with the control group. Have their reproductive capabilities been reduced?

Suggested research

- Investigate bioaccumulation and biological amplification as they pertain to pesticides.
- Read about the effect of pesticides and other toxic substances on the physiology of individual species. Thin eggshells are the most well-known example, but they are not the only ones.

11

Nitrogen fixation & acid rain

(The effect of acid rain on nitrogen fixation)

Nitrogen is the primary component of proteins and is important to all forms of life on our planet. Since 78% of the air we breath is nitrogen, you would think organisms would have access to all the nitrogen they ever need. It's not quite that simple, because *free* nitrogen in the air cannot be used by most organisms. For green plants to utilize nitrogen, it must first change form (be *fixed*). Life on the planet can thank a certain type of bacteria (and a few other types of organisms) for converting free nitrogen into a form that green plants can use. This process is called *nitrogen fixation*.

Nitrogen-fixing bacteria and a few fungi can use free nitrogen directly. The nitrogen is taken into their cells and converted into organic molecules. When the bacteria die and decompose, these organic molecules containing nitrogen are absorbed by plants, which can then incorporate them into plant tissues to be passed along food chains to higher forms of life.

Project overview

Most nitrogen fixation occurs as part of a symbiotic relationship between bacteria and legumous plants such as beans, clovers, and peas. The bacteria live in the roots of these plants which produce swellings, called *nodules*, around the bacteria. (See Fig. 11-1.) The bacteria use the nitrogen from the air (found in the soil) to survive. The nitrogen is converted into complex organic molecules. As the bacteria die, these molecules break down and are absorbed by the plant's roots so the plants can use the nitrogen. This symbiotic relationship and a sim-

72

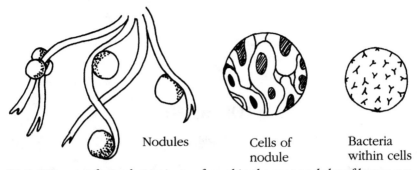

Nodules   Cells of nodule   Bacteria within cells

11-1 *Nitrogen-fixing bacteria are found in the root nodules of legumous plants.*

ilar type of relationship between some grasses and a nitrogen-fixing fungi are vital for life to exist on our planet.

All organisms have tolerance ranges within which they can survive. Factors such as temperature, moisture, sunlight, and nutrients must all fall within minimum and maximum limits. Rainfall in many parts of the country is far more acidic than normal. Rains often fall between 4.0 and 4.5 pH, even though normal rain is only slightly acidic, at about 5.6 pH. (See chapter 19 for more on acid rain.)

How does environmental stress such as acid rain affect the nitrogen-fixing capabilities of bacteria? Will acidified rain water minimize the nitrogen-fixing abilities of the bacteria enough to reduce a legume's ability to grow? Will it affect the growth of other nearby plants that depend on the legumes for nitrogen? Begin your literature search to find out about these and any other questions your research leads you to, and formulate your hypotheses. This project can be performed at any time because the materials can be purchased and the plants can be grown indoors.

Materials list

- Small packet of rye seed (a non-nitrogen-fixing plant)
- Small packet of inoculated clover seed. (These are seeds that have been inoculated with the nitrogen fixing bacteria. They are available from the supply houses listed in appendix B.)
- Nitrogen-free nutrient media to assure there is no source of nitrogen other than the clover mentioned above (also available from a supply house)
- Bag of vermiculite (an inert substrate for plant growth)
- 30 plant pots roughly 4×4 inches and a tray to accommodate them

- A balance
- Distilled water
- Gallon of a water solution with a pH of 4.0. (Ask your sponsor to create this for you.)
- Clear plastic wrap

Procedures

Rye grass (a non-nitrogen-fixing plant) will be grown under a variety of conditions:

1 With no nitrogen-fixing plants and normal pH water. (This group receives no nitrogen.)

2 With a nitrogen-fixing plant (clover) and normal pH water. (This group obtains nitrogen from the clover and receives simulated normal pH rainwater.)

3 With a nitrogen-fixing plant (clover) and distilled water that has been adjusted to a pH of 4.0. (This group receives nitrogen from the clover and receives simulated acid rain water.)

Prepare the 30 pots by filling each to 1 inch from the top with vermiculite (about 10 ounces each). Label 10 of the pots group A (no clover, normal rain). Label another 10 group B (clover, normal rain), and another 10 group C (clover, acid rain). (See Fig. 11-2.) Prepare the solution of nitrogen-deficient media plus normal rain by diluting according to the instructions that came with the media. If you are using the Ward's kit, mix with 4 liters of distilled water. This is used for groups A and B.

To prepare the solution of nitrogen-deficient media and acid rain, ask your sponsor to prepare a beaker of water adjusted to a pH of 4.0. Use this to dilute the nitrogen-deficient media for the C group. You're now ready to plant the seeds and begin the feeding program.

For the ten pots in group A (the rye grass alone), sprinkle 150 ml of nitrogen-deficient media plus normal water solution over the top of the vermiculite. (If the media is applied dry, add the dry media and then add 150 ml of distilled, plain water or amount specified with the media.) For the 10 pots in group B, the rye grass and the clover, do the same. For group C, sprinkle 150 ml of the deficient media plus acid rain solution. (Once again, if the media is applied dry, add 150 ml of the acid rain water or amount specified with the media.)

After all the pots have had the nutrient-deficient media plus water (either normal or acidic) applied, sprinkle 100 rye seeds evenly

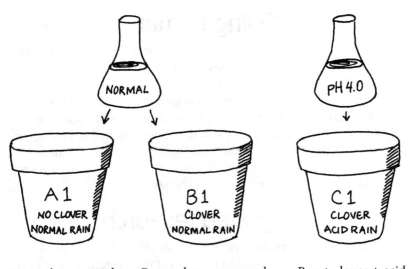

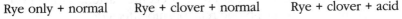

Rye only + normal   Rye + clover + normal   Rye + clover + acid

11-2 *Two solutions (in flasks) are used to water three groups of plants (A, B, and C). There are 10 pots in each group (numbered 1 through 10).*

over the surface of each pot. Then sprinkle 100 clover seeds (about a pinch) over groups B and C. Place clear plastic wrap over the pots. Place all 30 pots on a windowsill out of direct light. (You can use grow bulbs if you prefer, but all pots must receive the same amount of light.)

If the vermiculite dries out, add small amounts of either normal distilled water to groups A and B, or the acidic water solution (adjusted to a pH of 4.0) for group C. Make observations every two days. Take notes and measurements of the height, general growth, and appearance of each group. At the end of two weeks, make final observations and measurements. Cut the grass at the soil line and measure the weight of grass cut from each pot using a balance.

Analysis

Graph your data to clearly see the differences in growth. How important was the presence of clover (a nitrogen-fixing plant) to the rye grass in groups A and B? How did the acid rain group (C) do compared with the other two? Does it appear that regions experiencing acid rains might be loosing crop productivity because of its impact on the nitrogen-fixing process, or is it inconsequential?

Going further

- Continue a similar experiment, but test a range of pH levels. Establish a chart that represents the effect of various pH levels on nitrogen fixation.
- Investigate other forms of environmental stress on nitrogen fixation, such as increased UV radiation caused by ozone depletion, increased temperatures due to global warming, or electromagnetic radiation from high-tension power lines above vegetation. Or test the indirect effect of pesticides on the community of microbes in the soil.

Suggested research

- Research how environmental factors affect the growth of nitrogen-fixing plants. Do they affect the bacteria or the host plant, or is the symbiotic relationship affected?
- Study other nitrogen-fixing organisms, such as free living bacteria (as opposed to symbiotic forms) and fungi that are associated with grasses.

Plant stimulation & growth

(Does water, wind, and touch stimuli affect plant growth?)

Some gardeners claim that touching and talking to their plants improves their growth. If true, the ramifications could be enormous. Crop yields could be improved by inventing new machines that stroked or played recorded music to the vast fields of wheat and corn. This might sound far-fetched, but there is evidence that certain types of stimulation can affect the growth of some plants.

Plants grow and respond to their environment by way of four tropisms: phototropism, gravitropism, thigmotropism, and seismomorphogenesis. *Phototropism* is the bending of a plant towards light, which causes the stems to grow toward the light. *Gravitropism* causes the roots to grow into the soil for nourishment and the stems to grow toward the sky. *Thigmotropism* is a change in growth due to some form of contact such as touch. *Seismomorphogenesis* is the effect of a mechanical disturbance in the ground that affects the plant's growth. This project is primarily concerned with thigmotropism.

Project overview

In nature, plants are moved by the wind and struck by the rain, but greenhouse plants don't get this natural stimulation. If plants that are stimulated in nature grow better than those grown in an artificial environment such as a greenhouse, understanding the relation between stimulation and growth could have broad ramifications on greenhouse horticulture. Some research shows that touch results in shorter plants. Other research has shown that touching plants induces the release of ethylene, a gaseous hydrocarbon hormone that triggers defense mechanisms in some plants, resulting in the accelerated growth of either roots, leaves, or flowers.

Can artificially induced stimuli (wind, rain, and touch) improve the growth of Swedish Ivy (*Plectrantheus australis*) in a greenhouse environment? Will any of these three stimuli produce a healthier plant? Begin your literature search about these and any other questions your research leads you to, and formulate your hypotheses. This project can be done at any time of year because it is done within a greenhouse.

Materials list

- Access to a greenhouse. (This can be a large commercial greenhouse or a small temporary greenhouse built for this experiment. You might be able to borrow some space in a greenhouse for this project. Explain to the greenhouse proprietor that the experiment involves no insect pests or anything that can cause harm.)
- Enough Swedish Ivy plants to produce 60, 6-inch cuttings
- Rooting medium (purchased or made from two parts peat moss and one part sharp sand)
- Potting soil. (Mix two parts good-quality potting, one part peat moss, and one part sand.)
- 20 one-gallon clear plastic bags
- Large opaque plastic sheets. (Large plastic garbage bags will work fine.)
- Plant fertilizer (15-30-15, such as Miracle Gro.)
- Spray bottle
- Pruning shears
- Distilled water
- 6 plant (seedling) trays with holes in the bottom that can hold 10 plants each
- Soaker trays to retain water (enough to hold all the plant trays mentioned above)
- Feather duster (to produce touch)
- House fan (to produce wind)
- Wood rods attached to a base so they stand upright. (A large plastic garbage bag will be propped up by these frames to divide each experiment tray from the next.)
- Transparent plastic wrap
- A balance or an electronic scale
- Micrometer (to measure leaf thickness)
- Rubber bands

- A few automatic electric timers
- Garden hose and spray nozzle

Procedures

During the first part of the project, you must prepare a group of similar plant cuttings to be used for the control and experimental groups. Once the cuttings have taken root, they will be divided into groups and the experiment can begin.

To prepare the plants, place 4 inches of the rooting medium into each of the clear plastic bags. (These bags will be used to root the cuttings.) Make 60, 6-inch cuttings from the ivy plants. To make a cutting, slice the plants just below a leaf joint and strip the bottom leaf. Place each cutting 3 inches deep into the potting soil within the bags. Put three such cuttings into each bag as shown in Fig. 12-1. Press down on the potting mixture to make it firm enough to support the plants upright. Be sure the three cuttings are not touching one another or they will rot.

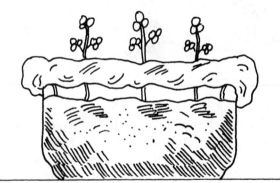

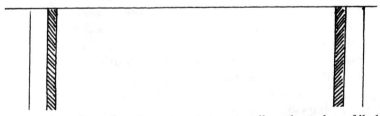

12-1 *Place three 6-inch cuttings into a 1-gallon plastic bag, filled with 4 inches of soil. Roll down the sides of the bag.*

Spray the plants within each bag just enough to wet them. Then pull the opening of the bag together and blow air into the bag so it becomes inflated. Seal the bag tightly with a knot and a rubber band.

(See Fig. 12-2.) Keep all the bags in the greenhouse so they get plenty of light and remain warm. After about one week, open up the bags and check the roots. They should be about 1 inch long. If they are too short, close the bag again and wait another few days until they are all at least 1 inch long.

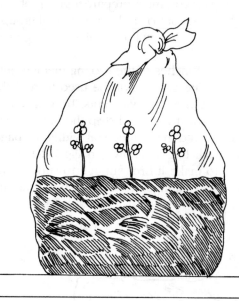

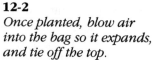

12-2
Once planted, blow air into the bag so it expands, and tie off the top.

Once all the roots have attained the proper length, begin rolling down the sides of each bag a little each day to allow the plants to become accustomed to the room temperature. This process should last about another week. The plants are now ready for potting. Fill the plant trays with the potting soil mixture and transplant 10 of the rooted cuttings into each of the six trays.

The trays must be separated with opaque plastic sheets about 3 feet high, as you see in Fig. 12-3. You can use wood rods, pvc pipes, or anything that can be attached to a base to stand upright and support plastic bags. Attach the plastic sheets to this frame to act as dividers. All the trays must receive the same amount of light and water. Document the amount of light they receive in the greenhouse. Is artificial lighting used? If so, for how long each day?

Next, prepare the plant food by mixing 1 teaspoon of Miracle-Gro for every 4 liters of distilled water. (You'll need one liter for each tray every other week.) The plants will be fed this solution every other week. You must also have enough plain distilled water to water all the plants once every other week. When feeding and watering the plants, pour the liquid into the soaker trays that contain the plant

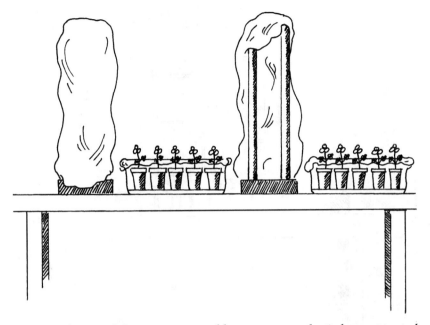

12-3 *Each tray of plants is separated by an opaque plastic bag supported by a stand.*

trays. This avoids having the water come in contact with the plants, which is one of the experimental factors.

The exact amount of food and water provided will vary depending upon the conditions within the greenhouse. Adjust accordingly, but always keep the amount consistent between all groups and document your procedures. Water (with distilled water) and feed the plants (with the Miracle-Gro solution) on alternate weeks (adjust as needed).

The six trays can now be divided into three project groups:

1 Touch stimulation
2 Water stimulation
3 Air stimulation

Each of the three groups contains two trays. One tray will be a control and the other exposed to the stimuli. Label each group and its trays. Now you must set up the appropriate apparatus for each group.

For the air stimulation group, place a fan two feet away from the first tray. (See Fig. 12-4.) The fan is left on for three hours every day. (Timers make this easier to manage.) The second tray is the control for this group and should receive no air movement at all.

For the water stimulation group, lay strips of plastic sheeting on the two trays to cover the soil. Crisscross these strips to create layers

12-4 *A fan produces wind for the air stimulation group.*

that will cause dripping water to drain off the strips and not be absorbed into the soil. (You don't want the water to be absorbed into the soil, since this would add another variable.)

Use a garden hose to spray water on one of the trays in this group for two minutes twice a day. Leave the second tray as a control, receiving no water stimulation. (It too should have the plastic sheeting applied for consistency.)

For the touch stimulation group, use a feather duster to touch the plants. Touch the plants in the first tray by lightly "dusting" each row of plants back and forth for three minutes each, twice a day. (See Fig. 12-5.) The second tray is the control and should receive no touch stimulation.

Continue watering, feeding, and applying the appropriate stimuli to each group over a period of six weeks. Keep diligent notes each day about what was done and when. Also, make general observations about the health of the plants in each group. Don't take any actual measurements, since this would act as a stimulus. At the end of the six weeks you are ready to take the final measurements to determine how the groups compare.

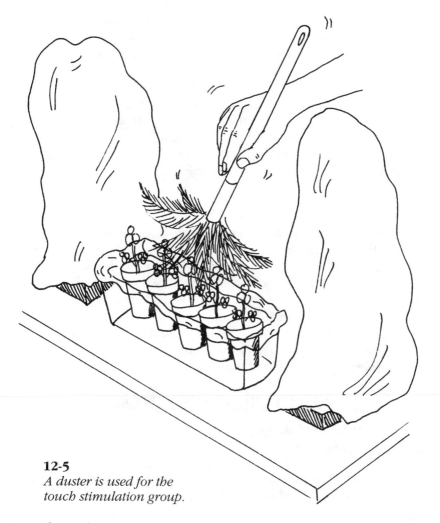

12-5
*A duster is used for the
touch stimulation group.*

If possible, consider doubling or even tripling the number of trays used throughout this project to improve the reliability of the data collected.

Analysis

Before beginning to take measurements, record your observations about the overall appearance of all of the plants. Then, measure the shoot length for each plant in all the trays. Next, measure the shoot diameter and get the average leaf thickness with a micrometer. Gently remove the plants from the soil and measure the root length. Clean off all the soil from the roots and measure the weight of the entire plant (shoots and roots). After the plants have dried, measure the mass of the entire plant once again.

Once you have collected the raw data, plot a graph for each of the trays. How did the trays within each group compare? Did the plants in the experimental trays grow better than the controls? Did the stimulation appear to help, hinder, or be unimportant to plant growth?

Once you analyze the data within each group, compare the groups. Did any one form of stimulation result in more growth than others? Does it appear that any of the forms of stimulation improve the growth of greenhouse-grown plants?

Going further

- Based on your results from this project, continue testing additional amounts of stimulation. For example, if you found that two minutes of touch, twice a day resulted in improved growth, set up the experiment to test two minutes of touch three, four, five, and six times a day. Is there a point of diminishing returns?
- Test the combination of some of these forms of stimulation. If touch and air produced minimal results, would there be a synergistic effect if they were combined?

Suggested research

- Study the latest developments in research about this field. Use recent journal articles for the latest news. There are also a number of books about this subject.
- Investigate how any positive results (improved growth due to stimulation) could be applied commercially.

Part 4

Energy:
For better
& for worse

In its broadest sense, *energy* is the ability to do work—the ability to produce a change in matter. Energy can be in the form of heat, light, electricity, motion, or in some chemical reaction. Fossil fuels are burned to release energy that we use to our advantage, such as gasoline to drive cars and coal to generate electricity in power plants. The first two projects in this section investigate two alternatives to fossil fuels: solar and wind power.

Some forms of energy, such as nuclear radiation, are harmful to life. The effects of some less-intense forms of energy, such as electromagnetic radiation, are just beginning to be thoroughly studied. One of the projects in this section investigates the effects of this radiation on bacteria, and another looks at how much radiation emanates from a personal computer and what can be done to stop it.

13

Solar energy

An alternative to fossil fuels

(Maximizing the efficiency of solar cells)

Throughout history, the rise and fall of civilizations has been linked to the availability of fuel. Since the turn of the century the world population has doubled, but our use of energy has increased 12-fold. This dramatic increase is due not only to more people, but also from a 30-fold increase in the number of products we manufacture and now depend upon to maintain a certain lifestyle.

Currently, about 80% of our energy comes from fossil fuels, which include coal, oil, and natural gas. Fossil fuels are considered *nonrenewable* because they are not replenished as rapidly as they are consumed. More important than their limited availability is the fact that they are the primary cause of air pollution today. Electric power plants and the automobile are the two biggest contributors to this environmental dilemma. Both use fossil fuels and belch forth a variety of pollutants into the air, contributing to air pollution, acid rain, and global warming.

In an effort to reduce our dependency on fossil fuels, alternative sources of energy are being researched and developed. Most of these alternative forms of energy are considered *renewable* because they are continually replenished, even when used extensively. Alternative energy includes solar power, hydroelectric power, geothermal power, wind power, and biomass power.

Project overview

Clean, safe solar power is often touted as the answer to all our energy needs in the future, replacing the environmentally damaging use of fossil fuels. The outlook certainly is hopeful, but the technology must still be delivered to make this a reality. Today only about 1% of the world's energy comes from solar power.

Currently, there are four ways to harness solar energy:
- Passive solar heating systems
- Active solar heating systems
- Solar thermal power plants
- Photovoltaic cells, commonly called *solar cells*

The first two are used to produce heat and hot water. Solar thermal power plants convert collected heat into electricity, while solar cells convert sunlight directly into electricity. Many believe solar cells offer the most exciting possibilities.

Solar cells were first developed in 1954 and became popular during the 1970s, when solar-powered pocket calculators became the rage. Solar power technology has enabled these cells to produce electricity for thousands of homes in outlying regions where it is impractical to tie into the electric power line grid. Most of these homes are located in remote regions of Alaska and villages in India. Although solar cells are still far too expensive to replace the use of fossil fuels, future advances can change this scenario quickly.

Solar cells are used today for a variety of devices from calculators to heating homes. How can you maximize the use of solar cells? At what angle should the cell be situated for the most efficient collection? How do weather conditions affect the collection capabilities? Begin your literature search for these and any other questions your research leads you to, and formulate your hypotheses. This project can be performed at any time of year.

Materials list

- Solar cell. (These inexpensive cells can be purchased at electronics stores, hobby shops, auto parts stores, or boat dealers.)
- Lamp bulb. (This bulb must have a compatible voltage rating with the solar cell. Buy them together to make sure they match. You'll probably use a small flashlight bulb.)
- Lamp socket to accommodate the bulb
- Multimeter or voltage meter

- Electrical wiring
- Protractor
- Two wooden boards to mount the apparatus. (One should be large enough to mount the solar cell, lamp socket, and multimeter. The other should be large enough to act as a base. See "Procedures" for details.)
- String
- Three eye hooks
- Hinge to attach the two boards and allow movement
- A few screws or nails for mounting

Procedures

The project consists of three parts. In the first, you determine a baseline for collection efficiency. In the second, you determine how the angle of the solar cell panel to the sun affects collection efficiency. Finally, you determine the impact of the sun's altitude on collection efficiency. All three parts should be repeated several times for verification.

To set up the apparatus, attach the solar panel, lamp socket, and multimeter to one of the boards as shown in Fig. 13-1. Once they are all attached to the board, wire the three devices as shown in the illustration. Now use a hinge to attach this board to the other board, which will act as a support, as in Fig. 13-2. Attach eye hooks, as shown in the

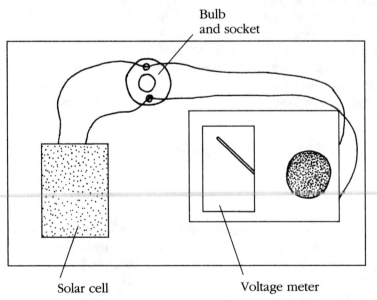

13-1 *The device board contains the solar cell, voltage meter, socket, and light bulb.*

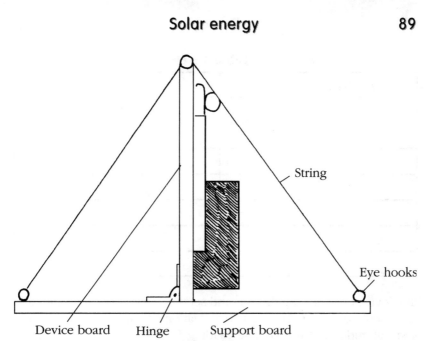

13-2 *The device board is mounted with a hinge to the support board. A string running through eye hooks is used to stabilize the apparatus.*

illustration, to the ends of the support board and the top of the device board. Tie a string to one eye hook, run it through the top hook and tie it off tightly at the other eye hook. This string will allow you to angle the device board (perpendicular board) while it remains stable.

Once the apparatus is put together, begin the first part of the project. Establish a baseline by taking the apparatus outdoors at noon on a clear, sunny day. Place the device on a table in the direction of the sun and angle the device board (using the hinge) so the solar cell is aimed directly toward the sun. Read the voltage reading on the multimeter. Then, use a protractor to measure the angle between the device board and the support board. This is the sun's *altitude.*

For the second part of the project, determine how the cell's angle to the sun affects collection. Be sure the panel is facing the sun. Use the protractor to set the angle of the device board at 10-degree intervals. Begin with 10 degrees from the vertical and go down to 10 degrees from the horizontal. For each observation, measure the voltage on the multimeter, the angle to the base, and the angle of the board to the sun. Enter this data into Table 13-1. (The "Power" column is discussed in the "Analysis" section.)

For the final part of the project, determine how the sun's altitude affects efficiency by taking hourly measurements from sunrise to sunset. Pick a day forecasted to be clear. Beginning at sunrise, position

Table 13-1

Angle with base	Angle with sun	Voltage	Power (V^2)

the device board facing the sun and set the angle to the sun's altitude, as described earlier. For each observation, document the time, the sun's altitude, and the voltage reading from the multimeter. Record the data in Table 13-2.

Table 13-2

Time	Sun's altitude	Voltage	Power (V^2)

Analysis

The power in an electrical circuit is determined by Joule's Law, represented by the equation

$$P = \frac{V^2}{R}$$

where V is the voltage (measured by the multimeter), R is the resistance of the lamp bulb (measured in ohms), which is a constant, and P is power measured in watts.

To analyze the data collected in the two tables, calculate the power and fill in the appropriate columns. (Be sure to calculate the power for the baseline as well.) This data can be illustrated by plotting the points on a graph. How does the angle of the solar cell to the sun affect the power compared with the baseline? How does the sun's altitude affect the power? Are the curves linear? How critical is the positioning of solar cells in creating electricity?

Going further

- Continue the experiment, using the same apparatus, but test for the impact of cloudy days. How about various types of clouds?
- Try the same experiment with the altitude of the sun, but keep the device facing south (instead of facing the sun). Take the readings throughout the day and compare the data with that collected in the third part of this project.
- Does temperature affect collection?
- Can metal reflectors increase the power?

Suggested research

- Investigate the use of innovative forms of solar power, such as solar thermal power plants and solar ponds.
- Investigate the use of other innovative energy sources, such as wave power and moon power.

14

Wind power

An alternative to
fossil fuels

(Maximizing the efficiency of windmills)

Fossil fuels (oil, natural gas, and coal) provide the majority of the world's energy supplies. Fossil fuel reserves and resources are limited and will someday become depleted, but there are two more important factors that make continued dependence on these fuels a gamble. First is our need to import vast quantities of oil, resulting in a supply that rises and falls with the coming and going of international crises. The second and more important factor is the environmental toll these fuels take on our planet.

Burning fossil fuels in power plants and automobiles is the primary culprit for many of our environmental problems. Global warming, air pollution, and acid rain all are caused to some degree by the combustion of fossil fuel.

Alternatives to these fuels do exist. They include nuclear power and a collection of renewable energy resources that replenish themselves and will never become depleted. Renewable energy, often called *cool energy* since they do not contribute to global warming, include solar, wind, hydroelectric, geothermal, and biomass energy. These forms of power are virtually pollution-free. A major shift to renewable energy supplies could reduce many of our most pressing environmental problems.

Wind has been harnessed by humans for centuries, but new high-tech innovations can make wind a major player in solving our modern environmental problems.

Project overview

Wind energy is air- and water-pollution free. It can convert about 90% of the available energy into useable energy, making it one of the most energy-efficient sources of power. Wind power is also cost-competitive with fossil fuels and is the least expensive of all the renewable energy sources.

Unfortunately, very little wind power is currently produced in the U.S. Almost all of it is in California, where it supplies about 1% of the state's needs. Many experts think the wind can supply about 20% of the U.S. energy needs within the next 20 years.

Today's *wind turbines* (they're no longer called *windmills*) work efficiently in areas that have average winds of at least 12 miles per hour at least 70% of the time. Technological advances are needed to make wind turbines generate electricity efficiently in sites receiving less wind. These moderate- and low-wind sites, as they are called, are the prime target for most of today's research and development on wind power.

Does the number of blades on a wind turbine affect the speed at which it will spin? Does a certain number of blades (two, three, four, six, or eight) work best in low-, medium-, and high-speed winds? Which combination of blades and wind speed produces the most energy? Begin your literature search about these and any other questions your research leads you to, and formulate your hypotheses. This project can be performed at any time of year.

Materials list

- About a dozen plastic pinwheels from a toy store, to simulate the wind turbines
- House fan with three speeds (to simulate the wind at varying speeds)
- Strobe light to measure the revolutions per minute of the fan and the pinwheels. (See if your school has one, or if your sponsor can procure one for this project.)
- Five small hobby motors that have permanent magnets. (These must be motors that can generate electricity. See "Procedures" for more detail. They can be purchased at a hobby or toy store for a few dollars each.)

- Ampmeter or multimeter that can read milliamps (Your school probably has a few, or they can be purchased at an electronics store or hobby shop. Additional meters would mean less work.)
- Five styrofoam thread spools to connect the axis of the hobby motor to the axis of the pinwheel
- Five flat pieces of wood to act as a base for the pinwheels (A piece of ¾-inch plywood about 1 foot square would work well.)
- Wooden dowels to support the pinwheel stick from bending in the wind and to support the motor.
- Scissors
- Glue
- Hand drill with bits the same diameter as the pinwheel stick and the wooden support dowels
- Five large metal alligator clips

Procedures

This project consists of two parts. In the first part, you put together five pinwheels with varying numbers of blades to simulate wind turbines and use a fan to simulate wind. A strobe light is used to determine which pinwheel spins the fastest at each of the three fan speeds. In the second part, you attach the axis of each pinwheel to the axis of each motor and the leads from each motor to a multimeter. This determines which pinwheel generates the most power at each of the three wind speeds.

To begin, create five different types of pinwheels. Remove the blades from the stick by pulling them off the axis, but don't damage the blades. Using these blades, create pinwheels consisting of two, three, four, six, and eight blades each. Cut off the unnecessary blades at the base or remove them completely if possible. Be sure all the blades are the same length and distributed equally throughout. (See Fig. 14-1.)

Once the blades are arranged properly, glue them together to maintain the proper spacing. After the glue dries, place the blades back on the stick axis. Spin them to be sure they move freely. To make it easier to use the strobe light, glue a small piece of brightly colored paper on one of the blades on each pinwheel. Make all the pieces of paper the same size and use the same amount of glue to attach the paper so this doesn't become a variable.

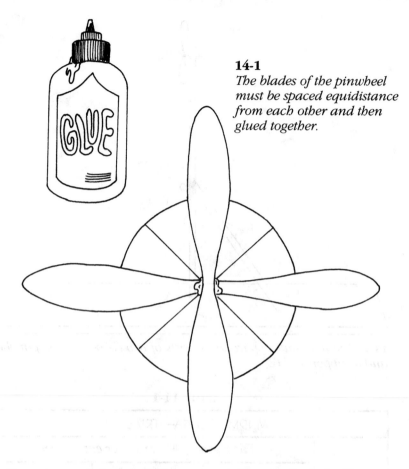

14-1
The blades of the pinwheel must be spaced equidistance from each other and then glued together.

To mount each "windmill" to a support base, drill a hole the same diameter as the pinwheel stick, into the middle of a plywood base. (See Fig. 14-2A.) Insert the pinwheel into this hole. Use a wooden dowel or rod (Fig. 14-2B) to help support the pinwheel and keep it from bending in the wind. To mount this dowel, drill another hole (Fig. 14-2C) at an angle so the dowel can be inserted into the base. Attach the other end of the dowel to the pinwheel stick with a metal alligator clip (Fig. 14-2D) or similar device as you see in the illustration. Repeat this procedure for the other four windmills.

You can now begin the experiment to determine which pinwheel will rotate the fastest at three different fan speeds. First, use the strobe light to measure the speed of the fan blades (in revolutions per minute) for each speed (low, medium, high). Learn how to operate the strobe by following the instructions that come with the device. Fill in Table 14-1 with these speeds.

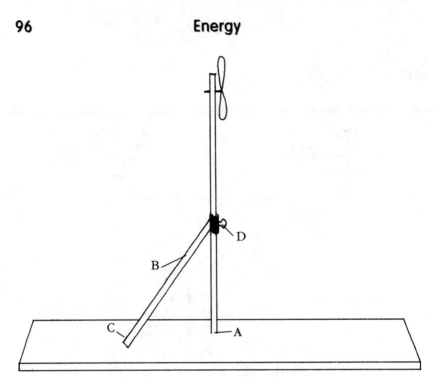

14-2 *The windmill apparatus consists of a base board, the pinwheel, and a support rod (B).*

Table 14-1

# of Blades	Fan Speed (fill in r.p.m. for each speed)		
	Low	Med	Hi
2	r.p.m.		
3			
4			
6			
8			

"WINDMILL" DATA—TRIAL ONE

After obtaining the fan speeds, place the two-blade windmill 3 feet in front of the fan. Run the fan at the low speed. Use the strobe light to read the speed of the pinwheel. Note the speed (in rpm's) in the table. Do this for each of the three speeds. Repeat this procedure for the other four windmills and continue to document the results. Now that you know which pinwheel in combination with which wind speed rotates the fastest, move on to the next part of the project to see which windmill and which wind speed produces the most power.

This part of the project requires that you mount a small motor to the pinwheels and attach a multimeter. To do so, attach a styrofoam thread spool to the back of each pinwheel axis as you see in Fig. 14-3. Insert the spool into the back of the pinwheel axis so it is firmly in place. You might have to glue it to remain fixed.

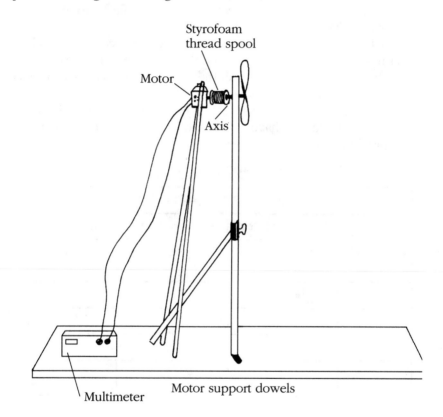

14-3 *Modify the existing apparatus (from Fig. 14-2) by adding a styrofoam spool, motor, motor support rods, and a multimeter.*

Next, attach the motor to the other side of the spool. Be sure to get the correct type of motor for this project. Most motors use a source of electricity such as a battery to turn an axis. In this project, the axis will be turned (by the pinwheels) which will then generate the electricity to be read on the multimeter. Only certain types of motors are capable of doing this. Be sure the motor you purchase contains *permanent magnets*.

To attach the motor to the spool, insert the axis of the motor into the spool so it remains firmly in place. To support the motor's weight and to keep it from moving, insert two more wooden dowels into the base at angles and secure it to the motor as you see in the illustration. Finally, attach the multimeter to the wires coming out of the motor. (If the wires aren't long enough, the meter will have to rest on a support.) The apparatus is now ready.

Place the first pinwheel 3 feet in front of the fan. Turn the fan on at low speed and read the milliamps as seen on the meter. Begin filling in Table 14-2. Do the same for the next two speeds. Once all the data has been collected for the first pinwheel, repeat this procedure for the other four and record all the data. Use the strobe light once again to read the speed of the pinwheels. The speed might have changed, since the apparatus has been modified with the addition of the motor. (If you only have one motor, you will have to move it from one pinwheel to the next for each test.)

Table 14-2

"WINDMILL" DATA—TRIAL ONE		
Fan Speed (fill in milliamps for each speed)		
# of Blades milliamps	Low	Med	Hi 2
3			
4			
6			
8			

Analysis

Which pinwheel had the highest revolutions per minute at the low, medium, and high fan speeds? Do more blades necessarily mean more speed? Does more wind mean more speed with all pinwheels? Which pinwheel generated the most electricity at each speed? Do more blades necessarily mean more electricity? Does more wind mean more electricity? What combination of blades and wind was the most efficient?

Going further

Create models of mountains or valleys and place the windmills at various locations throughout the simulated landscape. Determine how the geography of the land impacts the efficiency of your "wind turbines."

Suggested research

- Research those factors that will effect large-scale wind turbines, such as torque.
- Read the most recent literature to find the latest developments in wind power research and development.

15

Electromagnetic radiation

Our silent partner

(Does low-level EMR affect bacterial growth?)

Electrical circuits create both an electrical field and a magnetic field that radiate out from the devices containing the circuits. Personal computers, hair dryers, television sets, electric blankets, and high-tension wires all produce these fields. In many ways, magnetic fields created by electrical circuits are similar to magnetic fields created by a magnet. Both types of fields become weaker the farther away they are from their source; both pass through many types of materials and both cannot be perceived by humans.

The magnet's magnetic field, however, remains constant in a fixed direction around the magnet. The magnetic field produced by an electrical circuit, however, alternates direction. The circuit reverses itself 60 times a second (60 hertz) in the U.S. and Canada. Since these fields fluctuate at this low speed, they are said to be in the extremely-low-frequency (*ELF*) range.

Recent studies have shown the possibility of health risks associated with this type of radiation. The subject is very controversial, but since most of us are continually bathed in this radiation, many scientists feel it warrants further study. Some research has shown a correlation between exposure to this type of radiation and health risks such as some forms of cancer, childhood leukemia, and birth defects.

Project overview

Devices called gaussmeters are used to measure levels of electro-magnetic radiation. Surveys can be performed to see how much ELF radiation exists in a home or office. If these fields do pose a health risk, the fields can be reduced or even eliminated in many instances.

Many studies have been performed to see if there is truly a correlation between this ELF radiation and a greater incidence of health problems. Experiments that determine if this radiation is harmful to other forms of life can help us understand if these concerns are warranted. If lower forms of life such as bacteria or invertebrates are harmed, we know that additional studies should be performed and preventive measures taken when possible.

This project studies how electromagnetic radiation produced from common household appliances such as a television or personal computer can affect the reproductive capabilities of the common bacteria *E. coli*. This bacteria is normally found in our digestive tract. If radiation harms this bacteria, might it be dangerous to us?

Does electromagnetic radiation produced by common household appliances affect the reproductive capabilities of E. coli? Begin your literature search to answer this and any other questions your research leads you to, and formulate your hypotheses. This project can be performed at any time of year.

Materials list

- Spectrophotometer (This device measures the bacterial growth by determining how much light at a specific wavelength is absorbed. The more light is absorbed, the more bacteria is present. You can perform this experiment without a spectrophotometer. Speak with your sponsor about other methods of measuring growth that don't require instrumentation.)
- Gaussmeter to measure the amount of ELF radiation present. (One might be available in your school, or you can purchase or rent one from Fairfield Engineering, among other places, by calling 515-472-5551.)
- Small transformer and a home appliance such as a television or personal computer. (Any two small electrical devices that produce high readings on the gaussmeter can be used.)
- Culture of E. coli bacteria. (This common bacteria can be purchased from supply houses in culture tubes, agar plates, or as a freeze-dried inoculum. Nine culture plates are needed.

Cultures that come in slant tubes, broth tubes, or freeze-dried
will have to be prepared and inoculated onto the agar plates.)
- Nine culture plates
- Growth medium for E. coli

Procedures

Follow the instructions that came with the gaussmeter (Fig. 15-1) to
learn how to measure the amount of radiation emanating from various devices such as a transformer, a television set, and a computer.
Take measurements close to each device and then at varying distances from the device. Record your observations and note the exact
location that produced the highest readings for each device. For example, you might note "Computer monitor—5.5 reading at 1 inch,
front, center of screen." (See Table 15-1.)

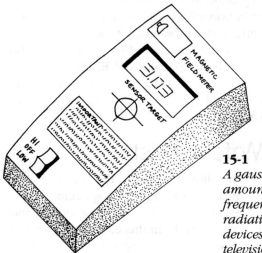

15-1
*A gaussmeter reads the
amount of extremely low
frequency (ELF) magnetic
radiation created by electric
devices such as computers and
televisions.*

Select the two devices that yield the highest measurements. They
will be used to study their effect on bacterial growth. (These devices
must be small enough to be placed on a table.) For the remainder of
these procedures, we'll be using a small transformer and a small television set, but you can use other devices.

Prepare three tables in a room at least 5 feet away from each
other. Two of them must have access to an electrical outlet. Use the
gaussmeter to be sure the space around the tables produces similar
readings before proceeding. All tables should be in similar conditions
regarding light, temperature, etc. No other electrical device should be
turned on in the room during the experiment.

Table 15-1

Device	Highest Reading (in milligauss)	Location
Television		
Computer	5.50	1" in front, center of screen
Transformer		
Electric blanket		

Place the transformer on one table and the television on the other. The third table has no equipment. You are now ready to place the E. coli cultures on these tables.

Your nine agar plate cultures must all be at the same stage of growth. Discuss with your sponsor the proper technique to transfer inoculum from the existing culture (either an existing agar plate, slant tube, or broth tube) to all nine agar plates. If you purchased freeze-dried inoculum, follow the instructions that came with the material.

⚠ **Warning!** Before working with live cultures, be sure to discuss safety precautions with your sponsor. This includes proper handling techniques and proper disposal of the cultures when the experiment is completed.

On the first table, place three of the culture plates near the transformer (or other device). Place them in the same location you noted received the highest gaussmeter readings. Place three other plates on the next table, near the television, once again at the location having the highest gaussmeter readings. (See Fig. 15-2.) Place the final three plates on the control table.

Once all three tables have been set up, turn on the transformer and the television (or other devices). If you are using a television, turn off the sound and turn the picture black, so these cannot be considered variables. Record the start time and any other useful information. After 24 hours, remove the plates and use the spectrophotometer (or other device or technique) to measure the amount of growth that has occurred. Be sure the plates are clearly marked, since they will be returned to the same location after taking your first set of readings.

In this experiment, a Spectronic 20 was used, with readings taken for 590 nm (nanometers) wavelength and a 20 nm (nanometers) slit

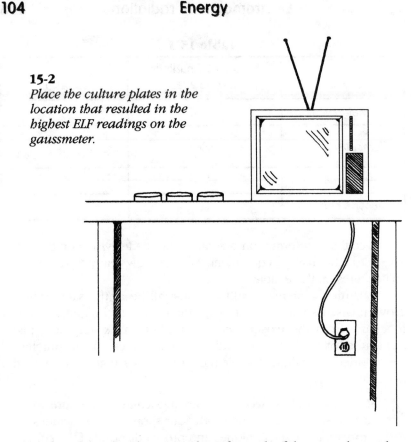

15-2
*Place the culture plates in the
location that resulted in the
highest ELF readings on the
gaussmeter.*

width. Record the absorbency readings for each of the nine plates. Place
the plates back at their proper locations immediately after your observations. Record the data in Table 15-2. Repeat your measurements at 48,
72, and 96 hours.

Analysis

How did the readings differ over time between the three groups? Did
those plates in the radiation fields experience less growth (lower absorbency readings) than the controls? Was there an inverse relationship between the amount of radiation present and the amount of
bacterial growth? Does it appear that ELF radiation has a negative effect on E. coli reproduction? Create a graph to illustrate your results.

Going further

- Run a similar experiment, but place the plates at various
  distances away from one of the devices. Does the growth rate
  increase as the amount of radiation decreases? Is there an
  apparent "safe distance" from these devices?

Table 15-2

Group	ABSORBENCY READINGS			
	24 hrs.	48 hrs.	72 hrs.	96 hrs.
Transformer Culture A	.280	.350	.510	.600
Culture B	.235	.320	.420	.525
Culture C	.290	.350	.480	.550
Television Culture A				
Culture B				
Culture C				
Control Culture A				
Culture B				
Culture C				

- Use different devices such as screens, paints, and other barriers to determine if they actually work in stopping ELF radiation. (Many such devices are advertised for use with personal computers.)
- Run a similar experiment, but use different organisms such as fruit flies to determine how ELF radiation affects their reproductive capabilities.

Suggested research

- Use the latest journals to research the most up-to-date studies on ELF radiation health concerns.
- Study the difference between electric field (E-field) radiation and magnetic field radiation. Look into how some companies that sell shields for personal computers are using these two types of fields to confuse customers.

16

Electromagnetic radiation & personal computers

(Measuring and controlling ELF radiation in PCs)

Personal computer displays, video display tubes (*VDTs*), and terminal displays, all of which are basically the same types of device, have been accused of posing health risks for many years. These displays, like any device containing an electrical circuit, produce electrical and magnetic fields that radiate out from the devices. Some recent studies have linked the magnetic radiation with a multitude of health problems, including cancer and birth defects. (There has been little research regarding the effects on health to the electrical radiation produced.) The magnetic radiation produced can be categorized as either extremely-low-frequency (*ELF*) radiation and very-low-frequency (*VLF*) radiation. Most of the studies linking health problems with magnetic radiation involve ELF radiation. (See Fig. 16-1.)

Since millions of people spend all day, five days a week in front of a personal computer or terminal, many individuals and companies are not waiting for more evidence about possible harm caused by this form of radiation. They are taking action they hope will protect those who use computers. A variety of technologies are sold that claim to reduce or eliminate the ELF radiation exposure produced by personal computers.

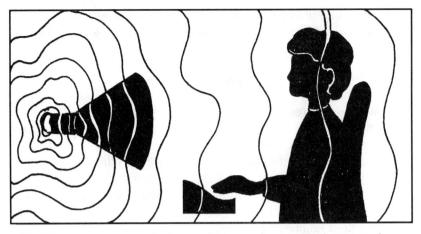

16-1 *Electromagnetic radiation radiates out from most electronic devices.*

Project overview

Inexpensive, hand-held devices called gaussmeters, or ELF magnetic field meters, can read electromagnetic emissions. Emissions are measured in units called *milligauss*. People can purchase or rent these devices to take emission readings around their personal computers as well as throughout their home.

In recent years, organizations have established electromagnetic emission standards. These standards dictate the maximum acceptable levels of electromagnetic radiation emanating from personal computers. The first standard, created by the Swedish government and called the *MPRII guideline*, sets maximum emissions at 2.5 milligauss at 0.5 meters from the front of the screen. Many people believed this standard to be inadequate protection. New standards have been set by a Swedish labor union, which has since been accepted by the New York City Board of Education. These standards, called the *TCO guidelines*, require a maximum of 2.0 milligauss at 0.3 meters from the screen.

Many personal computers meet these standards, but many do not. The only way to tell if a computer is within the guidelines is to take readings with a gaussmeter. If a computer is emitting excessive radiation, there are many devices available that claim to reduce these emissions.

Do personal computers in your school, home, or at a parent or friend's workplace meet the TCO emissions guidelines? If they do not meet these standards, are there methods that can reduce the emissions and put them into compliance with the standards? Begin your literature search about these and any other questions your research leads you to, and formulate your hypotheses. This project can be performed at any time of year.

Materials list

- Access to a number of personal computers. (You will take measurements on a number of computers, until you find one that produces excessive radiation.)
- Gaussmeter (These small hand-held devices are easy to use.) Check to see if your school has one. If not, it can be purchased or rented. Among places where gaussmeters can be rented or purchased is
  Fairfield Engineering
  P.O. Box 139
  Fairfield, IA 52556
  (515) 472-5551
- ELF Armour, optional. (This device is designed to reduce electromagnetic emissions. It is a steel alloy cylinder that fits over the neck of the display's cathode ray tube. It must be installed by a licensed television or computer repairperson. This device is also available from Fairfield Engineering.)
- Other devices designed or at least claiming to reduce electromagnetic emissions produced by computer displays, such as "anti-radiation" screens made of fine nylon mesh or glass. (Other devices such as sprays or paints can also be tested.)
- Ruler or measuring tape
- Ball of string
- Protractor

Procedures

The first part of this project involves taking readings with a gaussmeter around a personal computer to see if it meets the TCO standards for ELF radiation emissions. Measurements are taken until a computer is found that does not meet these standards. (This should not be too difficult to find.) The second part involves using a variety of corrective devices to see if they reduce emissions and bring the device into compliance with the standards.

To begin, read through the instructions that came with the gaussmeter. Familiarize yourself with the basic operating procedures. To begin taking readings, cut a length of string 0.3 meters (11⅞ inches) long. Place one end of the string up against the center of the screen and hold it out in front of the screen. Hold the gaussmeter so the end of the string is directly within the sensor position as indicated on the meter.

Since this radiation is directional, you must take readings with the meter turned three different ways as described on the meter. (See Fig. 16-2.) Turn on the meter and take your first reading. Rotate the meter 90 degrees, keeping the end of the string on the meter's sensor position, and take another reading. Rotate it once again and take a final reading.

16-2
Since electromagnetic waves are directional, the gaussmeter must be rotated in all directions.

Document the highest of the three readings. This completes the first of nine readings. Label this the "CC," or "Center-Center" reading. (See Fig. 16-3.)

To take the next two readings, measure 0.3 meters up from the first location. Take readings at this location and label it the "HC," or "High-Center" reading. Then measure 0.3 meters down from the first location and take three more readings, calling it the "LC," or "Low-Center" reading.

The next three readings are 22.5 degrees to the right of the first three and the last three readings are 22.5 degrees to the left of the first three. To take the remaining readings, first find the middle of the top

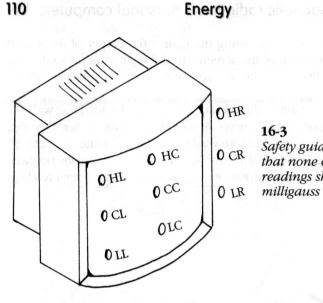

16-3
Safety guidelines dictate that none of these nine readings should exceed 2 milligauss (at 0.3 meters).

of the computer display by measuring its width and length. (See Fig. 16-4A.) Measure the distance from this center point to the front edge of the monitor (FIG. 16-4B). Add 0.3 meters to this distance. Cut a piece of string to this length. This number will be used as the radius of the arc, as you see in the illustration.

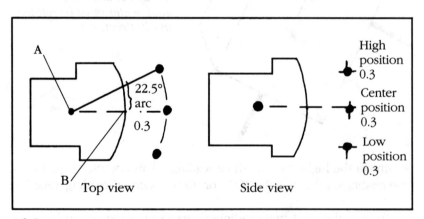

16-4 *To pinpoint where the readings should be taken, cut a piece of string and measure a 22.5° arc from the top center of the monitor.*

Hold one end of the string on the top center point (*A*) and hold the other end out in front of the display. Have someone hold the protractor and measure 22.5 degrees from the string. Rotate the string to this angle. The next three readings are taken from this angle. Take the first reading at this angle at the midpoint of the display and label these numbers as "CR," as shown in Fig. 16-3. Measure 0.3 meters up from this location and take the next readings ("HR"). Take the next reading down 0.3 meters from the original reading ("LR").

Take the final three readings in the same manner, but measure the 22.5 degree angle in the other direction. These will be CL, HL, and RL. You now have all nine readings. If any of these readings are above the maximum allowable levels of 2.0 milligauss, the display does not meet recommended levels. Repeat this procedure on a few other computer displays. Use displays that do not have any kind of protective screening or other devices used to reduce electromagnetic radiation.

After finding a display that does not comply (the more radiation the better), you can begin the second part of the project to compare a variety of anti-radiation devices. Try to locate some anti-radiation screens on computers at your school, home, or a parent's workplace. Some are made of a fine nylon mesh and others of glass. Install these on the computer to be tested and take the same readings as explained above. (If they don't fit properly, simply hold them in place and take the readings.) Document the results for each device.

Finally, after having tested the display with no form of protection and one or two screen type devices, have a licensed professional computer or television repairperson install the Armour ELF device into the display. (This portion is optional.) After it has been installed, take the same nine readings, adding this data to the table. Once the final readings have been taken, you can analyze the data.

Analysis

Of all the displays tested, what percentage had readings that did not comply with the TCO standards? How did the anti-radiation screens or other types of devices tested reduce these levels? What happened after the protective metal was installed?

Going further

- Use the gaussmeter to take readings throughout your house or school. Are there any "hotbeds" of ELF radiation?
- Modify this project to study how distance affects the radiation levels.

Suggested research

- Research the most recent literature about the health effects of electromagnetic radiation.
- Analyze the relation between marketing claims made about some anti-radiation devices and what they are capable of accomplishing.

Part 5

Aquatic ecosystems

Our planet is often called the water planet. With roughly 360 billion billion gallons of water believed to exist in our biosphere, the name is well deserved. Aquatic ecosystems include freshwater lakes and ponds, saltwater oceans, and other bodies of water with varying degrees of salinity called *brackish waters*.

Our streams, rivers, lakes, and other bodies of water have been used as toilet bowls for decades. This is probably because of the quantity of water that exists and the fact that it will "wash away" practically anything. For this reason, aquatic ecosystems are often the first to be harmed or destroyed by human intervention and many throughout the country and world are in a bad state of health.

This section includes projects that investigate heavy metal contamination, pollution caused by fertilizers and sewage, and the effect of acid rain and organic pollution on the most important producer in the water, algae.

17

Heavy metal contamination
Synergism

(Using the vinegar eel as an indicator of pollutants)

Bodies of water are continually used to dissolve, dilute, and otherwise rid ourselves of chemicals we no longer need. Thousands of different kinds of substances are used for manufacturing processes or produced as byproducts of these processes. Once these substances are no longer needed, they must be disposed of in some way. For decades the common method of disposal was simply pouring the brew of waste out an effluent pipe that simply dumped into a stream or other body of water. (See Fig. 17-1.) New regulations require that much of this waste be treated, but much of this direct dumping of untreated wastes still goes on. Even when treated, many of the hazardous components still remain to be released into the environment.

Heavy metals are some of the worst environmental offenders. Compounds containing metals such as lead, mercury, nickel, and copper are often found within this waste. These metals are toxic, even at very low levels, to most forms of life. Their existence is usually measured in parts per million (*ppm*). Even minute amounts of metals in aquatic environments can cause problems. The problem is made worse by the process of *bioaccumulation* in which toxic substances such as heavy metals are absorbed by organisms and remain within their bodies indefinitely. The concentration of these toxic substances increases over time until it reaches deadly levels.

114

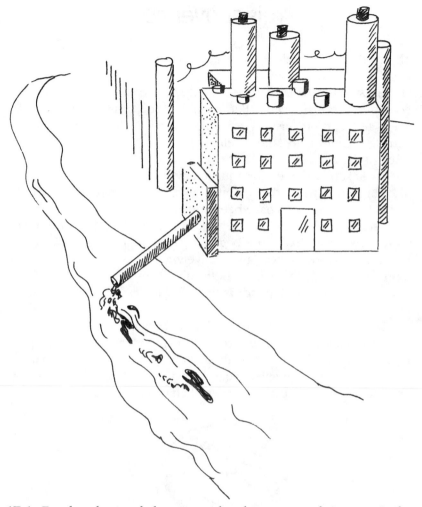

17-1 *For decades people have considered streams and rivers as "toilet bowls" to flush away wastes.*

The situation is made still worse by a process called *biological amplification* in which the toxic substances found within one individual are passed along food chains as they are eaten by other animals. For example, plankton within a lake absorb minute quantities of a toxic substance from the water and develop a high concentration within their tiny bodies. Invertebrates that feed on countless plankton develop still higher concentrations within their bodies, and fish that feed on the invertebrates develop still higher levels. This process continues to the top of the food pyramid—us.

Project overview

Aquatic pollution is a global concern with numerous ramifications. The earth is often called the water planet not only because of the abundance of water but also because of the importance of water to all forms of life. What happens to aquatic ecosystems affects other ecosystems in many ways. For example, food chains that transcend water and land organisms pass toxic substances from fish and other aquatic organisms to land-dwellers, including humans who eat the catch of the day.

Toxic substances in our aquatic environments are usually found in combination with other harmful substances. Although many individual toxic substances have been studied for their impact on aquatic ecosystems, studies about synergistic affects between two or more of these substances have just begun to gain momentum. We might know that two substances are relatively harmless to an ecosystem if found individually, but what if both substances happen to have been dumped into the same pond? Is there a synergistic affect that results in a deadly combination?

This project tests to see the effect of heavy metal pollutants on an aquatic organism (the vinegar eel). More importantly, it tests the positive synergistic affects, if any, these substances have in combination with one another. The vinegar eel is used as an *indicator organism*—one that is sensitive to environmental change. (See Fig. 17-2.)

17-2
The vinegar eel is actually a nematode, commonly found in aquatic ecosystems.

How do individual heavy metal pollutants affect the vinegar eel? Will any of the individual substances tested to be relatively harmless to the vinegar eel become harmful if found in combination with another? Begin your literature search to answer these and any other questions your research leads you to, and formulate your hypotheses. This project can be performed at any time of year.

Materials list

- A culture of vinegar eels, *Turbatrix aceti* (purchased from a scientific supply house)
- About a dozen well or depression slides
- The following chemicals, preferably in small dropper bottles (from a scientific supply house):
  - 1-molar aqueous solutions of aluminum nitrate, copper(II) nitrate, lead nitrate, and nickel nitrate
  - 0.25-molar aqueous solution of silver nitrate
  - 0.01-molar aqueous solution of mercury(II) nitrate

⚠ **Warning!** Acquire, work with, and dispose of these chemicals under the supervision of your sponsor.

- Sterile pipettes
- Distilled water
- Protective gloves
- Protective goggles
- Dissecting microscope
- Stop watch or watch with a secondhand
- Grease marker to label slides

Procedures

The project has two parts. In the first part you test the effect of individual pollutants on vinegar eels. In the second part you test for synergistic effects of these chemicals. Your observations are critical to the success of this project. Be sure to take detailed notes of the behavior elicited by the worms for each test. For example: How rapidly do they swim? In what directions do they swim? What types of movements do they make?

Use a pipette or an eyedropper to put two drops of distilled water in a well slide. Stir the vinegar eel culture thoroughly and place one drop from the culture into the well slide. Observe the behavior of these organisms under a dissecting microscope (or under low power on a compound scope). Watch them for a few minutes and take notes. Once you become familiar with their normal behavior patterns, move on.

Label each of the bottles containing the pollutants with a letter. Mark well slides with corresponding letters, so there is one slide per bottle. Use a sterile pipette or eyedropper to place one drop of distilled water and one drop of the vinegar eel culture into each well slide. Keep the size of the drop consistent.

⚠ **Warning!** From this point forward, be sure to wear protective eyewear and gloves, and work under the supervision of your sponsor.

Use a sterile pipette to place one drop of pollutant A onto well slide A. Immediately start the stopwatch and observe through the dissecting scope the behavior of the worms. (See Fig. 17-3.) Observe for five minutes. Be sure to make note of negative results as well (if there is no change in the behavior). Repeat this procedure for each of the pollutants to be tested.

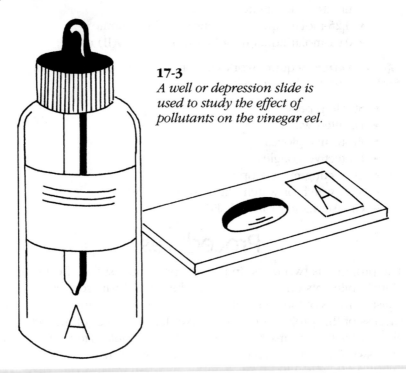

17-3
A well or depression slide is used to study the effect of pollutants on the vinegar eel.

Next, test to see if there are any synergistic effects when substances are combined. Use the mercury solution along with each of the other five substances to see which, if any, display positive synergy. Label five well slides with the numbers *1* through *5*. In your notes, relate each number to one of the pollutants with the exception of the mercury(II) nitrate. For example, slide 1 might refer to aluminum nitrate plus the mercury, and slide 2 might be copper(II) nitrate plus the mercury. (See Fig. 17-4.) Once you've labeled each slide, continue.

Place a single drop of the worm culture into each of the labeled well slides. For the first slide, add one drop of mercury(II) nitrate plus one drop of one of the other pollutants. Start the stopwatch and observe through the dissecting scope. Use the mercury(II) nitrate with each of the other solutions and take observations for each.

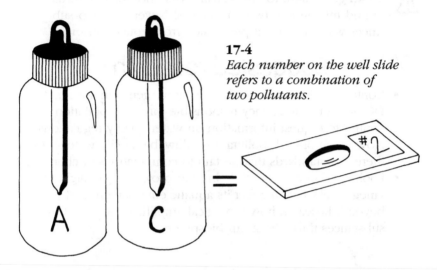

17-4
Each number on the well slide refers to a combination of two pollutants.

⚠ **Warning!** When you are finished with the entire project, check with your sponsor about proper disposal methods for the substances used.

Analysis

How did the individual pollutants affect the organism? Analyze the data and conclude which one caused the most harm and which the least. From the second part of the project, determine which combinations of pollutants caused the most harm and which the least. Compare the individual results with the combination results. Does it appear that some substances become more harmful when used in combination with others? Is there a synergistic effect with any two? If the vinegar eel is harmed by some of these substances, how might this have an impact on the local ecosystem?

Going further

Consider the vast array of different kinds of pollutants that are found in aquatic habitats. Use a similar experiment to test for synergistic tendencies between other types of pollutants commonly found in aquatic environments.

⚠ **Warning!** Be sure to check with your sponsor before using and mixing any two substances! Never mix two substances without explicit permission from your sponsor.

Suggested research

- Contact the Environmental Protection Agency in Washington DC or your state agency responsible for water pollution control to request information on water quality regulations. How much of each pollutant is allowable in city waters? Are there any standards that pertain to combinations of chemicals?
- Look beyond the well slide in your project. How might the vinegar eel's health affect its aquatic environment and beyond? Research how biological amplification spreads toxic substances throughout our biosphere.

Fertilizer, sewage & aquatic ecosystems

(The effects of fertilizers and sewage in aquatic environments)

Urbanization and large-scale agriculture have resulted in regions of the world where the volume of our wastes and agricultural byproducts have become major environmental problems. Sewage from cities and fertilizer runoff from large farms are responsible for nutrient enrichment of aquatic ecosystems. Although nutrient enrichment might at first glance sound like something good happening to the environment, it's not.

Natural ecosystems strike a balance between the amount of nutrients entering the system and the amount used by that system. The available nutrients are used by producers during photosynthesis and passed along food chains to consumers, only to be recycled as waste or when the organisms die and decompose. This supplies natural nutrients for another generation of organisms.

When human intervention changes the quantity of nutrients entering an ecosystem, equilibrium is lost and the natural order is destroyed. We change the quantity of nutrients entering an aquatic ecosystem in two ways: with sewage effluent and fertilizer runoff. Most of a city's domestic wastes and some industrial wastes end up being washed down the sink, toilet, or drainage pipe and entering into the municipal water system, where it is treated. The degree of treatment depends on the facility. Even the most advanced facilities, which are few, still allow large quantities of the nutrient-rich waste to make its way into a body of water for final dilution.

   This sewage is rich in nitrogen in the form of ammonia and nitrates, both of which exist in nature, but not in excessive amounts. Until recently, the sewage has also been rich in phosphates used in detergents. (See Fig. 18-1.) Phosphorus is an important nutrient found in limited amounts in aquatic ecosystems. Even small amounts of phosphorus added to an aquatic ecosystem can have a dramatic affect.

18-1
Laws have been passed to reduce the amount of phosphates dumped into the waste stream.

   Nutrient enrichment of aquatic habitats is also caused by fertilizer runoff. Fertilizer used for agriculture and for domestic use on lawns and golf courses is obviously rich in nutrients. Only a small portion of the fertilizer applied to the soil makes its way into the soil. The rest simply runs off after precipitation and makes its way to bodies of water where it adds to nutrient enrichment.

Project overview

The normal succession for any freshwater body is to gradually increase the nutrient load and the complexity of the inhabiting food web. Over long periods of time, a deep coldwater lake containing few organisms becomes a shallow, warm body of water with tremendous plant and animal diversity. After thousands of years, most ponds and small lakes will completely fill in with organic matter and become part of the land.

When this process occurs naturally, it is called *natural eutrophication*. When human activities alter this natural progression, by adding large amounts of sewage and fertilizers into an aquatic body, it accelerates this natural process and is called *cultural eutrophication*. Nutrient enrichment is often responsible for *algal blooms*, in which various forms of plankton experience population explosions, engulfing most of the surface waters of a lake.

This project is designed to study how nitrates, phosphates, and a combination of both affect an aquatic ecosystem. This is done by surveying algae, which is an excellent indicator of the state of an aquatic ecosystem. How do excessive nitrates effect natural algae populations in various bodies of water? How do excessive phosphates effect natural algae populations? How about a combination of the two nutrients? Is there a synergistic effect? Begin your literature search about these and any other questions your research leads you to, and formulate your hypotheses. This project is best performed during warm weather.

Materials list

- Mixture of potassium phosphate and water to simulate phosphate contamination (See below).
- Mixture of potassium nitrate and water to simulate nitrate contamination. (Both this and the potassium phosphate mixture can be made in the laboratory, under the supervision of your sponsor, to simulate actual concentrations of the pollutants from sewage and from fertilizer runoff. Alternatively, the solutions can be purchased premixed from Ward's. See appendix B. This project assumes you're using Ward's Solution.)
- 21 clear containers such as plastic cups or drinking glasses
- Marker or labels to identify each container
- Two eyedroppers or pipettes
- Paper toweling
- Access to three (or more) standing bodies of freshwater. (These can be lakes, ponds, or reservoirs. The more diverse they are, the better.)
- Sterile quart jars with lids to collect water samples
- Although this project only calls for visual observations of the condition of the water samples, more detailed analysis would require a dissecting or compound microscope. (See chapter 20 for details on analyzing algae samples.)

Procedures

Collect fresh water from each of the three bodies of water and place each in a sterile quart jar. Label each jar with the location, date, and time of collection. Be sure to take each sample using the same technique and from the same portion of the water, such as scooping the water from the surface down to a depth of 4 inches. When you get back to the lab, label three sets of seven plastic cups *1* through *7.* Label each set of cups with one of the three bodies of water. For example, you might have 1 through 7 "Ruby Lake," 1 through 7 "my backyard pond," and 1 through 7 "the swimming hole." (See Fig. 18-2.)

RUBY LAKE

1

BACKYARD POND

1

SWIMMING HOLE

1

18-2 *You'll have three sets of seven plastic cups. Each set contains water from a different location.*

Place 90 ml of water from each collection site into each of the server cups. For each of the three cups labeled *1,* add nothing since this will be the control. Add nine drops of the phosphate solution to the *2* cups. To the *3* cups, add 18 drops of the same. To the *4* cups, add nine drops of the nitrate solution. To the *5* cups, add 18 drops of the same. To the *6* cups, add nine drops of the phosphate and nitrate mixture. To the *7* cups, add 18 drops of the same.(If you're using homemade solutions, ask your sponsor what volumes to use.)

Once all the cups are ready, place some paper toweling over the tops and place them all in a sunny part of the room. All the cups must receive the same amount of light. Make observations about all the cups and begin to fill in a table similar to Table 18-1. Subjective visual observations, such as "light" or "dark green color" or "very cloudy" are sufficient at this time.

Each day for 10 days, add the same number of drops into each cup and make observations. As you make your visual observations, compare each cup to the control. After day 10, take final visual observations. At this time, you should analyze the algae populations both in numbers and in diversity to determine how each pollutant affected the natural populations, as indicated by the condition of the control cups. (See the "Procedures" section of chapter 20 for instructions.)

Analysis

How did each type of pollutant and each concentration affect the algae growth, both in diversity and in numbers? How did the nitrate alone, the phosphate alone, and the two together affect algae growth? Does one have more impact than the other? Is there a synergistic effect when combined? Does the concentration appear to make a difference?

Did the pollutants affect each of the three bodies of water in the same way, or are some types of ecosystems less likely to be harmed? How might the changes you observed affect the entire ecosystem in the region?

Going further

- Try to determine the actual effect of localized fertilizer use. For example, find a pond adjacent to a lawn or a farm that often has fertilizer applied. Perform water analysis of the nitrogen content to see if the nitrate levels are abnormally high. Then quantify the algae populations.
- Do the same type of experiment, but include water obtained near water treatment facilities. Compare them with other "unencumbered" streams.
- Perform a similar experiment, but add the acidity of the water as a variable. How does acid rain affect the nutrient enrichment? Does it accelerate or reduce the effects of nutrient enrichment on a body of water?

Table 18-1

OBSERVATIONS FOR RUBY LAKE						
Cup						
	#1	#2	#3	#4	#5	#6	#7

Day	#1	#2	#3	#4	#5	#6	#7
1							
2							
3							
4							
5							
6							
7							
8							
9							
10							

Suggested research

- Survey the literature for statistics about the actual impact of nutrient enrichment on natural ecosystems. How prevalent is it? How many bodies of water have been affected? What has been done to remedy those already affected? Has this remediation worked?
- Investigate recent local, state, and federal legislation controlling the use of phosphates in detergents. Has legislation helped solve the problems?
- Look into water treatment-plant technologies. How does primary, secondary, and tertiary treatment affect the release of these pollutants?

19

Acid rain & algae

(Killing our lakes)

Acid rain, more appropriately called *acid deposition*, weakens and kills trees, stunts the growth of many crops and other plants, and damages, if not destroys, entire aquatic ecosystems. Acid deposition is formed by a series of events. When fossil fuels are burned, they release many substances called *primary pollutants*, which include sulfur dioxide, nitrogen compounds, and particulate matter.

As these pollutants float through the air, the sun enables them to react with each other, creating sulfuric and nitric acids. These acids are called *secondary pollutants*. Both types of acids are picked up by droplets of moisture and then fall to earth with precipitation. These acids lower the pH of precipitation; hence the name, acid rain.

Normal rain has a pH of about 5.6, which is slightly acidic. Acid rain in New England and parts of adjoining Canada often receive rain with a pH of about 4.3, which is the acidity of grapefruit juice. Some mountain tops in New Hampshire have recorded rains with a pH as low as 2.1, which is about the same acidity as lemon juice.

Since the primary and secondary pollutants are carried by the winds, the resulting acid rain may fall far from where the fossil fuels were originally burned, making this a truly global problem.

Project overview

Probably the most serious damage caused by acid rain can be seen in aquatic ecosystems where watersheds accumulate the acidity. Aquatic ecosystems are intricate and fragile, with most organisms having limited tolerance ranges, meaning they are unable to handle fluctuations of most environmental factors, such as pH. Harm done to one species often ripples throughout the entire closed ecosystem rapidly.

Phytoplankton are the prevalent producers for many bodies of water. These organisms can act as indicators of forthcoming problems because they are sensitive to environmental change. What happens to these producers will affect the entire food web in short order.

How do acidified waters affect the quantity and diversity of algae present? What populations of algae are found in lakes or ponds in your area, and what is the pH of these bodies of water? Can a survey of algae within a body of water be used as an indicator of acidification? Begin your literature search to answer these and any other questions your research leads you to, and formulate your hypotheses. This project is best performed in warm weather.

Materials list

- Access to at least three lakes or ponds in your area
- Three containers, each capable of holding 5 liters of water (You can use multiples of smaller containers, such as five 1 liter bottles.)
- Plankton collection net that includes a collection bottle or tube (See "Procedures.")
- Large bucket to catch the water as it passes through the collection net
- Beakers to hold 100 ml of water
- Plankton-counting device or a compound microscope (See "Procedures.")
- Algae identification book (See appendix B for titles.)
- pH strips or other method of measuring the pH of water samples
- Three samples of lake water with each representing different degrees of acidification (normal with a pH of 6 to 7, endangered with a pH of 5 to 6, and acidified with a pH of 4 to 5) with representative sample populations of algae (These samples will act as standards for each level of acidification. Since collecting these samples would be difficult, they can be purchased from supply houses listed appendix B.)

Procedures

This project involves two parts. For the first part, you use purchased lake water samples that typify normal, threatened, and acidified lakes, and identify the types and numbers of algae present in each. This allows you to establish a standard of the types and numbers of algae found in lakes with varying degrees of acidification. For the second

part, you survey the algae found in your local bodies of water and
test the pH to see if they fall within the standards set in the first part.

Begin by surveying the algae and other plankton present in each
of the three samples of lake water you purchased. Identify as many
as possible and perform counts of these samples. (See Fig. 19-1.) Use
a book that illustrates and describes all forms of algae. Identify as
many genera as possible for each of the three samples and document
your observations.

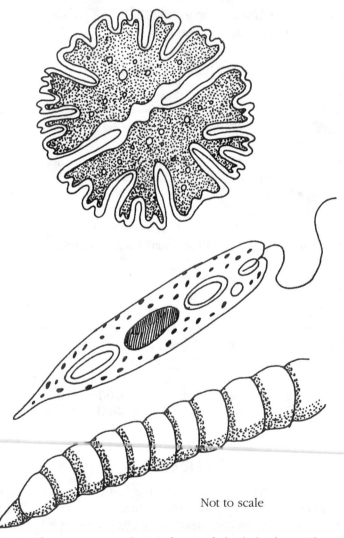

Not to scale

19-1 *There are many diverse forms of algal plankton. These
are just a few selected forms.*

Once you have completed identification, begin to count the numbers of each type present in each sample. There are many methods of counting algae. Some require nothing more than a compound microscope and some graph paper, while others require sophisticated equipment that can be expensive, such as the Sedgewick-Rafter Counting Cell or the Palmer Counting Cell. (See appendix B.)

Simpler methods are more tedious and less accurate but still useful and only require a microscope, preferably with a stage micrometer. In this method, a known volume of a sample, such as 1 ml, is placed under a standard cover slip (22×22 mm). Place graph paper beneath the slide. Count the organisms in one (vertical) field of vision across the entire width of the coverslip, using the graph paper as a guide. Repeat this procedure five or six times. Then use the graph paper to calculate how much of the 1-ml sample was counted to determine how many individuals are found per milliliter. (See chapter 20 for more details on this procedure.)

Once you have identified and counted the relative numbers of algae in each of the three standard samples, you can begin collecting your own samples from local lakes and ponds. There are a variety of ways to collect water samples. There are tow nets with metering devices that measure the amount of water passing through while filtering out and collecting the plankton. A simpler, less expensive method is to pour a known quantity of collected water through a net fine enough to allow the water to pass through but to collect the plankton in a bottle or tube. The instructions that follow assume you are using this simple type of device.

Collect 5 liters of water from each of the three bodies of water in your area. Be sure the collection vessels have been sterilized before beginning. Collect the water from near the surface, and remain consistent in your collecting technique at each site. Bring the samples back to the lab. Set up the collecting net as you see in Fig. 19-2. Before beginning the filter process, use your pH test strip paper, or other pH measuring device, to measure the pH of each sample. Document these results.

Once the pH is measured, slowly pour the 5-liter sample into the collection net. As the collection bottle or tube containing the organisms fills, pour the contents into a 100-ml holding beaker. Continue this process until all 5 liters have passed through the net. When finished, top the holding beaker off with distilled water to reach the 100-ml line. Label each beaker. (See Fig. 19-3.)

Once you have your 100-ml samples from each of the three bodies of water, identify and count these samples as you did in the first

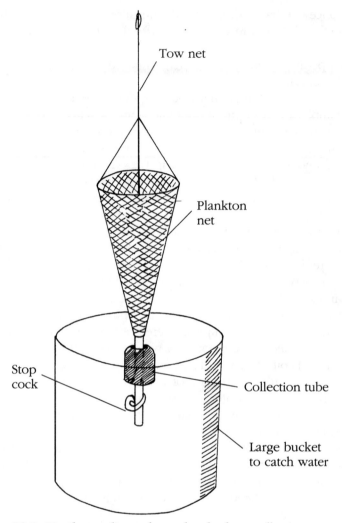

Tow net

Plankton
net

Stop
cock

Collection tube

Large bucket
to catch water

19-2 *Use the tow line to hang the plankton collection net upright, so the water samples can be poured through.*

part of the experiment. Compare the types and numbers of algae found in your local lakes with those you found in the standard samples you purchased.

Analysis

To help analyze your data, create graphs to illustrate your raw data. How did the diversity of the algae and the numbers of each in the purchased samples differ between the normal, endangered, and acidified lakes? Which has the most diversity and which the least?

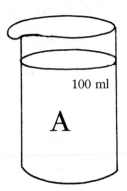

Filtered through
collection net

19-3 *Five liters of collected water is poured through the collection net, resulting in a 100 ml concentrated sample.*

What is the pH of the lakes or ponds in your region? Does this fall into the normal, endangered, or acidified lake range? Did the diversity and numbers of algae collected in your samples correspond with those found in the standard? For example, if the samples taken from your local lake had a pH of 5.5, did it contain the same kinds of algae with similar counts as the endangered lake standard, which has a pH in 5–6 range?

Does the diversity of algae and their relative numbers appear to be an indicator of the acidic condition of a lake?

Going further

- Continue this research by simulating varying degrees of lake acidification and observing the effect on a wide variety of aquatic organisms. Set up five large beakers or jars and add

500 ml of spring water to each. Adjust the water in each
vessel to create a series of pH levels between 6 and 3.5.
Collect or purchase a wide variety of aquatic organisms
including aquatic insects, crustaceans, and protozoans. Mix
the collection thoroughly and then divide it into five equal
parts. Add each part to each of the five beakers. Check each
vessel for diversity and number of organisms every hour and
then the next day. How do they compare in diversity and in
numbers over time?

- If your classroom is online with students in other parts of the
country (or world), ask you computer friends to collect water
samples from their local lakes and ponds and take readings
to include in your research.

Suggested research

- Investigate the existing literature about acidified lakes and the
impact to the local ecosystem. Find studies that have
followed the remediation of an acid lake.
- Read about other effects of acid rain, such as on crops and
buildings.
- Investigate what other factors affect the presence of various
types of algae in water.

Nutrient-enriched waters & algae

(Using algae to determine levels of organic water pollution)

All lakes and ponds are gradually filling up with organic matter and will someday become dry land through the process called *natural eutrophication.* Over long periods of time, usually thousands of years, large quantities of sediment containing organic matter are naturally washed into bodies of water with rain runoff from the local watershed. This enriched sediment provides nutrients for plant life to grow and establishes aquatic food chains and food webs. As this flora and fauna dies, it too, adds to the nutrient enrichment of the waters and accelerates the process.

As the sediment builds up, the waters become more shallow until sunlight can penetrate to the bottom, enabling emergent plants to root themselves and break through the water's surface. Nutrient enrichment slowly turns a deep, clear, cold lake containing few nutrients, called an *oligotrophic lake,* into a shallow, warm, and cloudy lake, rich with nutrients, called a *eutrophic lake.*

Over time, the large supply of decaying organic matter feeds vast populations of algae. As the algae and other organisms die, bacteria have a population explosion of their own, feeding on the decaying algae and other organic matter. Bacteria can deplete the water of its oxygen content and cause the collapse of the ecosystem and the death of the lake. The lake begins to dry out, becoming what is often called a *wet meadow.*

Project overview

Natural eutrophication is often affected by human intervention, compressing what might naturally take thousands of years into a few decades. When we cause this to occur, the process is called *cultural eutrophication.*

Eutrophication is accelerated because many human activities speed up the nutrient enrichment process. When fertilizers from agriculture, golf courses, and neighborhood lawns are applied, most of it is carried away with runoff water from rains, down gullies, streams, and rivers, into ponds and lakes. In some parts of the country, livestock wastes or sewage are also carried into the waters.

The introduction of all of these organic substances enriches the water at levels that would not normally occur for thousands of years, if ever. These excessive levels of nutrients often result in algal blooms that can stifle all other life. Bacteria decompose the decaying algae, reaching such large populations that they use up all the oxygen in the waters, killing larger organisms and resulting in a dead lake. Most algae cannot survive in waters containing low levels of oxygen, but some not only live in these organically polluted waters, but thrive in them.

Is it possible to use the numbers and diversity of algae present in a lake or pond to indicate the degree of organic pollution present? If so, can you determine the amount of organic pollution (nutrient enrichment) present in lakes and ponds in your local area by surveying the algae? Begin your literature search about these and any other questions your research leads you to, and formulate your hypotheses. This project should be performed during the warm summer months.

Materials list

- Access to three (or more) lakes or ponds in your area (preferably with varying degrees of eutrophication)
- Plankton-collecting net (You might be able to borrow one from your school or a local university, or you can purchase one from a supply house.)
- Nine closable, 1-liter jugs for collecting water samples
- Large bucket to catch the water as it passes through the plankton net
- Compound microscope (40X to 100X)
- Microscope slides and coverslips
- Graph paper (1-mm squares)

- Two pipettes (0.1-ml graduations)
- Nine 1000-ml beakers
- Nine 100-ml beakers
- Parafilm or plastic wrap
- Distilled water
- Iodine (or other special fluid designed to slow down protozoans, sold through supply houses)
- Algae identification guide (See the bibliography for suggestions.)

Procedures

This project involves collecting water samples from three local ponds or lakes, preferably ranging from oligotrophic to eutrophic conditions. These three samples will be analyzed for algae diversity and numbers. You then use a standard pollution index to determine the degree of organic pollution in each site and attempt to devise your own index.

Collecting your samples

You will collect three 1-liter samples from each site and filter out the algae, resulting in concentrated samples of 100 ml each. Begin by going to the first pond or lake. Use a closable, 1-liter container to scoop water from the surface. Fill the container and close. Take at least three such samples at each site. Keep your collecting technique consistent for all samples at all the sites. Make your collections from all three sites and return to the lab.

To filter out the algae and create a concentrated sample, set up your plankton net as you see in Fig. 19-2, (in the previous chapter). Most nets have a tie line for being dragged through the water. Use this line to hang the net upright. Tie it to a stand or some other fixed object above. Let the net hang down into a large bucket that can hold the net and the water as it passes through, as you see in the illustration.

Once the net is ready, slowly pour the first sample out of the collection jug into the collecting net. The algae and other plankton will accumulate in the collecting tube at the bottom of the net, but the water will pass out of the net into the bucket. As the collecting tube fills with plankton and other organisms, dump the contents into a 100-ml holding beaker labeled with the name of the site. After pouring the contents of the collection jugs through the net, top off each beaker to the 100-ml line with distilled water. Cover each beaker with parafilm or plastic wrap and poke with a few small holes through the wrap.

You should now have three 100-ml samples, one from each site. Now you are ready to begin the identification and counting portion of this project.

Identification and counting samples

There are many methods available to count algae and other plankton. Some use specialized and expensive devices such as the Sedgewick-Rafter Counting Cell or the Palmer Counting Cell. If these devices are available at your school, speak with your sponsor about using them. A simple technique, described here, requires only a compound microscope. (This procedure can be further simplified with a stage micrometer.)

Begin by acquainting yourself with the various types of algae. A few are shown in the previous chapter in Fig. 19-1, but use an algae identification guide for more detail. Use a pipette to take one drop from one of the samples and place it on a slide. Place a coverslip over the drop. Begin with a 40X-power microscope to survey the organisms. Try to identify each. After becoming familiar with most of these algae forms, begin the formal identification and counting process.

Cut a piece of graph paper composed of 1-mm squares to the same size as a coverslip. (Most coverslips are 22×22 mm.) Place the graph paper on a microscope slide and cover with a coverslip. Position the slide and the graph paper under the scope at 40X. Observe how many blocks of graph paper are visible horizontally and vertically in a single field of vision. (See Fig. 20-1.) You now know how much of the entire coverslip is visible in one field of view at that power. Repeat this process for 100X magnification also, and record the data.

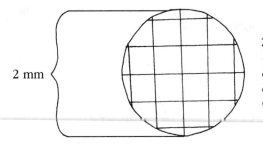

2 mm

20-1
Use graph paper to determine how much area is visible through one field of vision.

Gently stir each concentrated sample of algae to distribute the organisms evenly. Use a pipette to take a sample from the first beaker and drop 0.1 ml on a microscope slide. Place a coverslip over the drop to distribute the sample evenly beneath the slip. Position a thin strip of graph paper just beneath the microscope slide as shown in Fig. 20-2 to act as a reference.

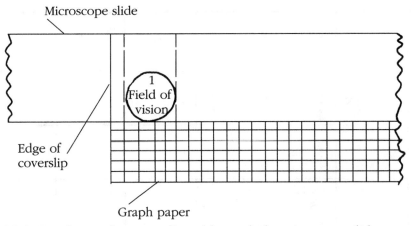

20-2 *Use the graph paper, aligned beneath the microscope slide, as a reference for counting cells.*

Begin counting individual algal cells that appear within the field of vision at the far left edge of the coverslip, as you see in the illustration. Check off in Table 20-1 each type you see. Algal colonies or filaments should be counted as a single unit. If mobile cells (such as the euglena) are difficult to count, take a 10-ml sample from the 100-ml beaker (after stirring thoroughly) and add one drop of iodine, which will kill the organisms and stain them. Stir this 10-ml sample thoroughly before removing the 0.1-ml drop to be observed.

After you finish counting a field of vision, move to the right one field of vision and continue counting. Continue until you are at the right edge of the coverslip and have completed counting an entire strip. (See Fig. 20-3.) To count another strip on the same slide, turn the slide around and repeat this procedure by counting the opposite edge of the coverslip. Repeat this procedure by creating another slide from the same sample and counting two more strips (bottom and top edges) so you'll have four strips counted for each sample. Repeat this procedure for each of the three samples taken from each of the three sites. You should now have columns A through C filled in the table.

Analysis

After tallying up all the numbers, determine the number of individuals (of each genera) per ml found in each of the original 100-ml samples collected. To do this, perform the calculations shown in the remainder of the table. The first row of the table has an example.

Table 20-1

A Algae type	B Number of cells / Strip #1	#2	#3	#4	C Total cells counted	D Total area counted (beneath coverslip)	E Total area beneath coverslip	F Equation $\frac{C}{D} = \frac{\text{Unknown}}{E}$	G Cells in .1 ml (beneath coverslip)	H Cells in 1 ml (from sample) G×10	I Cells in original collection H×100	J Cells/1 ml from entire collection 300
Oscillatoria	IIII IIII II	IIII IIII III	III IIII	IIII IIII IIII	50	2×22 mm/strip 8×22 mm/4 strips 176 mm²	22×22 mm 484 mm²	$\frac{50}{176} = \frac{X}{484}$ $\frac{50\times484}{176}=137.5$	137.5/.1 ml	1,375	137,500	458.3/ml

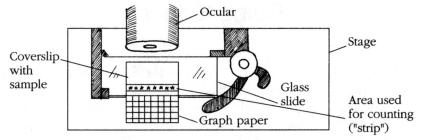

20-3 *Count across the width of the coverslip. This is one "strip." A stage micrometer makes the counting process easier.*

For example, assume 50 units of Oscillatoria were counted in your four strips. Since each strip (field of vision) covers 2×22 mm, all four strips cover 8×22 mm. You know, then, that 50 units were found beneath 176-mm squares. (See column D in the table.)

If there are 50 units per 176 square mm, how many are under the entire coverslip, which is 484 square mm (22×22 mm)? This equation

$$\frac{50}{176} = \frac{x}{484}$$

can be calculated as

$$\frac{50 \times 484}{176} = 137.5$$

You now know that there are 137.5 cells of this algae in the 0.1 ml of sample placed under the coverslip.

If there are 137.5 units in 0.1-ml, then there are 1,375 in 1 ml and 137,500 in the entire 100-ml sample you filtered out of the collection net. Since the 100 ml sample was concentrated from 300 ml originally collected at the lake, this number (137,500) must be divided by 300 to determine how many units were originally collected at the lake, per 1 ml. This is calculated as

$$\frac{137,500}{300} = 458.3$$

units of this algae per ml from the original collection sample.

Figure out the density for each type of algae in all the samples. Graph the results for analysis. In your literature search, look up the Palmer Pollution Index and see how the bodies of water you studied rate with this index. Investigate which forms of algae are tolerant of pollutants and which are not. Once you have determined how the water fits into the Palmer Pollution Index, research newer methods and indexes for measuring organic pollution levels that take other factors, such as pH, into consideration.

Going further

- Try to develop your own aquatic pollution index and rate the lakes and ponds in your area according to this index.
- Study the history of each lake in your area to determine what types of pollutants might have found their way into these bodies, or what natural processes might have led to cultural eutrophication.

Suggested research

- Research the most recent developments in using algae and other organisms as indicators of water pollution using the latest scientific journals.
- Look into the most recent technological advances regarding aquatic pollution detection.
- Study how *BOD* (biological oxygen demand) plays a part in the health of an aquatic ecosystem.
- Read about succession and how natural eutrophication figures into the process.

Part 6

New solutions to old problems

Some problems are "as old as the hills." New technologies are providing new ways to deal with some of these old problems. Some technologies, such as using beneficial insects to control harmful insect pests, is a tried, tested, and true answer to an old problem. The first two projects in this section study different aspects of biocontrol methods.

Other technologies are still in their infancy with regard to providing real answers to real old problems—such as making it rain when we want, instead of when nature wants it to. The last project in this section studies the effect of air pollution on seeding the atmosphere with a natural protein to induce precipitation.

21

Biocontrol
Predators, parasites, & parasitoids

*(Using parasitoid wasps and the
preying mantis as biocontrol agents)*

When it comes to farming and putting food into our mouths, insects have always been a nemesis to mankind. Throughout the world, and especially in developing nations, a great deal of the food grown never makes it into people's mouths because insects eat it first. Farmers continually battle insect populations to grow their crops. They use a number of weapons in this fight, primarily synthetic chemical pesticides. Resistant strains of plants are also used, as well as *biocontrol* (also called *biological control*). Biological control has become a state-of-the-art method of fighting insect pests without using harmful chemicals.

Some insects kill other insects. These beneficial insects can be successfully used to help control insect pests. The beneficial insects are called *biocontrol agents*. Using these biocontrol agents can keep pest insect populations down while reducing the farmer's dependence on synthetic pesticides. It can also save the farmer the cost of these expensive pesticides.

Reduced use of pesticides also means less chance of the consumer ingesting these substances, since they often remain on food as residues. As our environmental awareness about pesticide use increases, the use of biocontrol agents becomes more popular.

There are three kinds of biocontrol agents now being used to control insect pests:

- *Predators* attack, kill and eat other insects. The preying mantis and ladybug (beetle) are examples of predators. Predators kill and eat many insects throughout their lives. The insects eaten are the *prey*.
- *Parasites* live on another organism and feed on it, but don't usually kill the organism, called a *host*. A parasite may live on more than one host during its lifetime. Mites, for example, often parasitize insects.
- *Parasitoids* feed on only one host their entire life and usually end up killing the host, but only after the parasitoid has matured. There are many tiny parasitoid wasps that kill insects. (They are, however, harmless to humans.)

Before any biocontrol agent can be used, it must be thoroughly studied and understood. This is partly to ensure that the beneficial insect will actually control a certain pest, but also to determine the impact—both good and bad—of introducing large numbers of a new (exotic) organism into an ecosystem.

Project overview

This project entails studying two types of biocontrol agents: the preying mantis, which is a well-known predator, and a tiny parasitoid wasp. You will study important aspects of the lives of these insects to see how well (or poorly) they work as biocontrol agents. The two parts of the experiment can be performed in either order. You will collect data about each part, analyze the data individually, and then compare the data from both parts.

Parasitoids and biocontrol

One wasp that is frequently used for biocontrol in greenhouses is called *Trichogramma minutens*. (It doesn't have a common name.) This wasp is an *egg parasitoid*; the adult female wasp lays its eggs in another insect's egg. (See Fig. 21-1.) The immature wasp hatches out of its egg (within the host egg) and eats the inside of the host egg for nourishment. When the immature wasp is fully grown, it emerges out of the host egg as an adult wasp. The host eggs die.

Trichogramma is used as a biocontrol agent because it lays its eggs in a common garden pest, the tobacco (also called tomato) hornworm. Your experiment determines how effective this agent can be in controlling the tobacco hornworm pest. How long does it take for the parasitoid wasp to emerge as an adult from within the egg? How many wasps can emerge from one parasitized egg? How many eggs can a single wasp parasitize? What percentage of all the pests are killed?

21-1
*Parasitoid wasps often
oviposit their eggs into a host
insect's eggs.*

Predators and biocontrol

The preying mantis is probably the most common biocontrol agent. (See Fig. 21-2.) They are often released in gardens to kill pests. You will perform a series of experiments to determine how effective this biocontrol agent can be in controlling an insect pest.

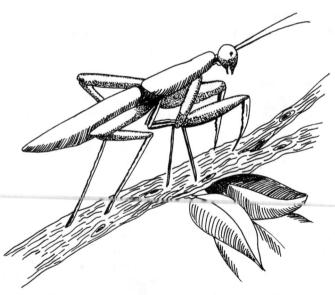

21-2 *The preying mantis is probably one of the best-known beneficial insects.*

How many offspring are produced by a single egg mass? How many offspring can a single female produce over her lifetime? How many insects can a single newly hatched mantis eat in a week? How many insects can a mantis destroy over its lifetime?

Begin your literature search about these and any other questions your research leads you to, and formulate your hypotheses.

Materials list

For the parasitoid part of the experiment (These wasps are visible to the naked eye, but they are very small, so most of the work is done under a dissecting microscope or a high-quality magnifying lens.):

- 10 tobacco (also called tomato) hornworm eggs, parasitized by Trichogramma minutens (purchased from a scientific supply house or possibly an organic gardening nursery)
- 10 deep saucers (about ½ inch high and 4 inches in diameter) that can be closed, or petri dishes with tops
- Fine forceps
- Small paintbrush (such as those used for model planes)
- Honey
- Spoon
- Dissecting microscope or high quality magnifying glass

For the predator part of the experiment:

- Preying mantis egg case. (You can order these from scientific supply houses or buy them at an organic gardening store. Or, with some luck, you can collect one outdoors.)
- Fruit flies to feed the preying mantis. (These, too, can be ordered from a supply house, or you can collect them by leaving a piece of fruit to rot outdoors in warm weather. You can collect them with an aspirator when they land on the fruit.)
- Other small insects, such as aphids and leaf-eating caterpillars, which can be caught in the field. (These will be fed to the preying mantis, as well.)
- One large, wide-mouthed jar (approximately 32 oz)
- Three small, wide-mouthed jars (approximately 16 oz)
- Nylon material to fit over the mouths of the jars
- Rubber band to fit around the mouths of the jars
- Cotton balls
- Transfer aspirator

Procedures

The procedures are divided into two sections: parasitoids and predators.

Parasitoids

This experiment can be done at any time in the year. First, you need to determine the number of wasps that emerge out of a single parasitized hornworm egg. Put a single parasitized egg in each of the 10 dishes. (Parasitized eggs are dark-colored. Don't use green eggs; they aren't parasitized.) Be careful separating the egg from the egg mass. Use either a fine forceps or a fine brush. (See Fig. 21-3.)

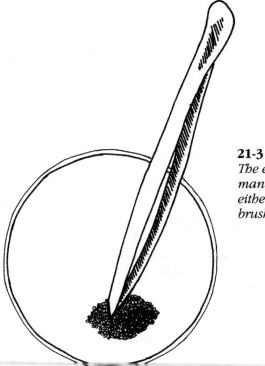

21-3
The egg mass must be manipulated carefully with either a fine forceps or a fine brush.

Place a small drop of honey in each dish. (The honey drop should be as small as this capital O.) Close the dish and seal it with scotch tape so the wasps cannot escape. (If they do escape they won't hurt anything, but your experiment will be ruined.) Keep the dishes at room temperature.

Each day, check each dish for adult wasps. They are small, so look at the dish with the magnifying glass or a dissecting microscope. (Look around the honey drop, since the first thing they will do after emerging, is eat.) Continue to observe them every day for four weeks. When they emerge, count the number of wasps in each dish. Note your observations for each dish throughout the four-week period.

Continue the experiment to find out how many eggs a single wasp can parasitize by using a few of the wasps that emerged in the last part of this experiment. In another set of dishes, place five, 10, and 50 unparasitized hornworm eggs. Place a single female wasp in each dish. Female wasps don't have hairs on their antennae (you'll need the dissecting scope to see this) and they don't move around very much, compared with the males. Use a tiny paintbrush or a transfer aspirator to pick up and move the wasps. You can tell when an egg has been parasitized because it will darken and turn black or brown in one or two 2 weeks.

Count the number of dark eggs to find out how many eggs a single wasp can parasitize. After the eggs turn dark, allow them to hatch. Once again see how many wasps emerge out of the eggs in each of the three dishes.

Predators

You can do this part of the experiment any time of year if you are ordering the insects, or from late summer to spring if you are collecting your own. Put the preying mantis' egg case (along with the stem it came on) in the large jar and keep the jar at room temperature. Cover the jar with the nylon material and hold the nylon on tightly with a rubber band. Cut a small cross in the nylon material, and then stick a wetted cotton ball halfway into the jar. (See Fig. 21-4.) This will be the insect's water supply. You can add water by dripping it onto the outside of the cotton ball when it becomes dry. Be sure there are no openings between the cotton ball and the nylon material.

Every day, check to see if the young have hatched. Once they hatch, count how many there are. (They will all emerge within a few hours of each other.) You can open the top to count them, since they cannot fly away. (You might want to put the jar in the refrigerator for about three minutes to slow them down before opening the jar.) How many emerged from a single egg case?

Now that you know how many offspring one female can produce, try to determine how many insects a preying mantis can eat. Since these insects will eat one another, separate two individuals from

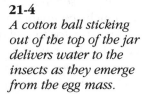

21-4
*A cotton ball sticking
out of the top of the jar
delivers water to the
insects as they emerge
from the egg mass.*

the others for this part of the experiment. Set up two smaller jars in a
similar fashion to the larger jar, with the cotton ball in the top of the
nylon mesh cover. Place a few twigs in the jars so there is a place for
the insects to land.

Now, place 10 fruit flies in each jar containing a single preying
mantis. To do this, suck 10 fruit flies into a transfer aspirator from
their container. Hold your finger over the hole of the aspirator so they
don't escape. Remove the cotton ball from the nylon and place the aspirator into the hole where the cotton was located. Blow to push the
fruit flies from the aspirator into the jar. Replace the cotton ball.

Every day, count the number of fruit flies in the jars. Make note of how many are left each day. Replace those that were eaten each day so you maintain 10 fruit flies in the jars. Do this for at least two weeks to determine how many fruit flies a young preying mantis eats per week.

Continue the experiment by keeping some of the preying mantises alive for two to three months. How long before the insects have developed into full-grown adults? Keep feeding them fruit flies. When they get bigger, switch to house flies or some other larger insect. Keep them alive for as long as possible. Compare the number of insects an adult preying mantis eats to that of a newly hatched mantis. Calculate how many it would eat over its lifetime. Then calculate how many insects all the preying mantis from a single egg case could theoretically eat during their entire lives.

Analysis

First consider what happened with the parasitoids. How long did it take before the adult emerged from the parasitized eggs? How many wasps can come out of each egg? How many eggs can a single wasp parasitize? Can you estimate how many insect pests can theoretically be destroyed over a given period of time from one female wasp? Draw a chart that plots the population growth curve of a population of parasitoid wasps. How many wasps emerged out of the second set of dishes containing five, 10 and 50 eggs? Calculate how many emerged from each egg for each dish. Chart the results.

Now, consider the results from the predator part of the project. How many young emerge from the preying mantis egg mass? How many fruit flies can each individual eat over a two-week period? If you continued to keep the preying mantis alive for a few months, how much can an individual eat over its lifetime? Can you calculate how many insects could be eaten from the offspring of one egg mass over the life of all the offspring?

How effective do you think these insects are as biocontrol agents? How do the parasitoids compare with predators?

Going further

- These experiments exclude all mortality factors such as disease, predation, and weather. Devise an experiment that would take mortality into consideration. Consider actual field studies.

- Try to determine what other specific types of insect pests can be controlled using these two biocontrol agents.
- In many cases, biocontrol is used in an area where chemical insecticides are also sprayed. How does the use of chemical insecticides affect the ability of a biocontrol agent to kill pests? Can you devise an experiment to test this?

Suggested research

- Read more about other biocontrol agents that have been used to successfully control insect pests. There are many others.
- Contact farmers or distributors who produce organically grown fruits and vegetables. Find out what they use for pest control.

22

Parasitoids
Behavior & pest control

(Studying the egg-laying behavior of a parasitoid wasp)

Parasitoids are insects that lay their eggs in other insects. Parasitoid insects can be used to control insect pests, reducing the amount of dangerous pesticides used. The parasitoid is called a biocontrol agent and the parasitized insect is the host. The immature (parasitoid) insect emerges from its egg inside the host and gets its nourishment by eating the host. The host dies and the parasitoid eventually emerges from it.

Lifecycles of biocontrol agents must be studied to thoroughly understand how the insect will fit into the ecosystem and to see how (and if) it survives.

Project overview

Parasitoid wasps are often used as biocontrol agents. These tiny wasps are harmless to humans. Some species lay their eggs (*oviposit*) in the host's pupal stage, others in the host's larval stage, and still others in the eggs of their host. (See Fig. 22-1.) One important aspect of a parasitoid's lifecycle is the female's egg-laying behavior. This behavior can affect the insect's success (or failure) as a biocontrol agent.

There is usually a direct relationship between the size of a female insect and the number of eggs she can lay. Since these wasps are very small, they have a limited number of eggs they can produce and must be selective about where they lay their eggs. Laying eggs in the wrong kind of host, a sick host, or a host that has already been parasitized means their eggs have less of a chance for survival. If the female parasitoid is to avoid wasting eggs, she must be able to sense the condition of a host to determine the chances for the survival of her offspring.

153

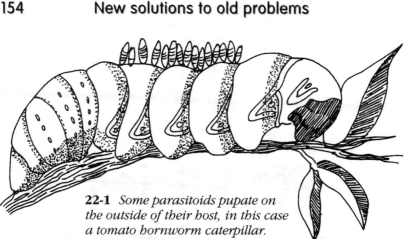

22-1 *Some parasitoids pupate on the outside of their host, in this case a tomato hornworm caterpillar.*

How does a mother parasitoid wasp sense the conditions of a host? How does she determine where to lay eggs? Does her selection criteria change under crowded conditions? Begin your literature search about these questions and any others your research leads you to, and formulate your hypotheses. This experiment can be done at any time of the year.

Materials list

- At least 50 newly emerged, female *Trichogramma minutens* wasps. (These can be purchased from a supply house or possibly from an organic gardening nursery. Sexing these insects is explained in the Procedures section.)
- About 70 tobacco (also called tomato) hornworm eggs to use as hosts for the wasp eggs. (These must be ordered from a supply house.)
- One petri dish with a top (or a covered dish about ½ inch deep and 4 inches in diameter)
- Fine pin
- Forceps
- Marker
- Small paintbrush (such as those used for painting model planes)
- Dissecting microscope or high-quality magnifying glass

Procedures

This experiment consists of two parts. In the first part, you compare the oviposition (egg laying) behavior of a parasitoid wasp on "good" versus "bad" host eggs. The next part is a similar test, but determines how over-crowded conditions change the insect's oviposition behavior.

Take about 20 hornworm eggs and gently squeeze them with the forceps until they become distorted, or put a hole in them with a pin. (You'll need to do this under magnification.) Draw a line with a marker to divide a petri dish into two halves. Label one half "good" and the other "bad." (See Fig. 22-2.) Place the bad (damaged) eggs on one side and an equal number of good (undamaged) eggs on the other side of the petri dish. Keep the good and bad eggs separated in the dish.

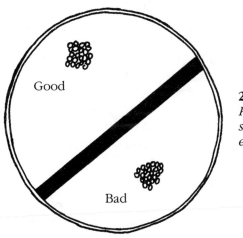

22-2
Place 10 "good" eggs on one side of the line and 10 "bad" eggs on the other side.

Now, add five female Trichogramma minutens wasps into the dish. Use the paintbrush to pick up and move the wasps, but be very gentle since they are delicate (or use a transfer aspirator as described in chapter 21). Females do not have hairs on their antennae (use a dissecting scope to see this), and they don't move around as much as males. As you place each wasp into the dish, close the top.

Observe the wasps' behavior under magnification. Watch how the wasps prepare to lay eggs. How do they walk over the eggs? Record their movements on each type of egg (good and bad). Record how they touch each type of egg. What body parts do they use to in-spect the eggs? Do they lay any of their eggs in the bad host eggs? How much time do they spend on the good eggs versus the bad? Watch the wasps for about one hour (observe for ten minutes out of every 20 minutes). Be sure to document differences between both types of eggs. Once these observations are completed, move on to the next part of the project.

For the second part of the experiment, divide a petri dish into two halves once again with a marker. Damage about 15 tobacco hornworm eggs as described earlier. Place 15 good eggs on one side of the dish and 15 bad eggs on the other side. Place 40 female wasps into the dish and replace the top. Begin your observations of their behavior. Make your observations as you did in the first part of the experiment. How does their behavior differ when the females are in overcrowded conditions?

Analysis

What conclusions can you draw from your observations? Does the female know what she is doing, or does she leave the young's fate to luck in the first part of the project? What parts of her body are used during her investigation of the host eggs? Does it appear as if she can tell a good egg from a bad egg? What happened when the number of good eggs became limited?

Compare your observations between both experiments. Does overcrowding change the oviposition behavior? How might these results affect the use of these insects as biological control agents?

Going further

- Devise an experiment to determine the actual density of ovipositing females to available eggs that elicits a difference in behavior.
- Devise an experiment to determine if environmental factors such as temperature affect the wasp's oviposition behavior and ability to reproduce.

Suggested research

- Read about how these and other types of parasitic and parasitoid wasps are used as biocontrol agents.
- Research what other factors (besides overcrowding) might play a role in using parasitoids as biocontrol agents.

Ice-nucleating bacteria

Let it rain

*(Does particulate matter affect the
ability of ice-nucleating protein to freeze water?)*

Our biosphere consists of two components: the *biota*, which is the living world, and the *abiota*, which consists of all the nonliving factors such as the geology of the land, the abundance of water, and the climate of a region. The abiota has considerable control over living organisms, dictating where they can and cannot survive. Technology is beginning to give the human race the ability to gain some slight control over parts of the abiota. Weather is one such factor that has the potential to be manipulated in some small ways, such as attempting to produce precipitation during an extended dry spell.

Inorganic substances, such as silver iodide, have been used with moderate success to cause precipitation. Organic substances, such as natural proteins found in some bacteria, have also been used to produce precipitation and can have far-reaching environmental applications, including preventing frost damage on crops, natural cooling, and water purification.

Project overview

Water freezes when enough energy (heat) is lost and water molecules slow down enough to align themselves in a lattice structure to form crystals. *Ice nucleators* are substances that help this process along.

They can be inorganic substances, such as dust and silver iodide, or organic substances, such as a protein. Ice nucleators attract molecules of water; in doing so, the molecules slow down. This allows them to form the lattice structure. *Seeding clouds* is a phrase often used to describe the process of artificially introducing ice nucleators to promote precipitation.

A natural ice nucleator protein was discovered in a strain of the common bacteria *Pseudomonas syringae*. This protein, called *INP* for *ice nucleating protein*, has been used successfully for snow-making purposes as well as other applications. The protein can be produced in concentrated form by a process similar to freeze-drying the bacteria.

When water has been seeded with INP, the molecules attach themselves to the protein and arrange themselves in a lattice structure, even though the temperature is not low enough for this to occur naturally. Once the process has begun, other molecules use this seed as a site to which they attach themselves. The result is the formation of ice crystals at temperatures well above normal freezing conditions.

Water freezes more rapidly when any of the ice nucleating substances (dust, silver iodide, INP, etc.) are present. How much of a difference is there between how long it takes for water to freeze with no nucleator and with INP present?

Many regions are often clouded by air pollution containing particulate matter, such as ash from fossil-burning power plants. What would happen if INP was seeded in areas with high concentrations of particulate matter? Is there a synergistic effect if two nucleators such as ash and INP are present, or do they negate one another? Begin your literature search to answer these and any other questions your research leads you to, and formulate your hypotheses. This project can be performed at any time of year.

Materials list

- One pack of INP (ice nucleating protein, available from scientific supply houses)
- Three microplates with four rows of 10 depressions. (These are plates that have rows of many small depressions similar to multiple-depression slides or well slides. You could also use a larger number of smaller microplates, such as six microplates with two rows of 10 depressions.)
- Two test tubes
- Graduated cylinder
- Two graduated pipets (10 uL)
- Aluminum foil

- Beaker of distilled water
- Thermometer that reads between –30°C and 50°C
- Stopwatch or watch with a secondhand
- Freezer (This project can be performed with any freezer. It would be best, however, to prepare the freezer so you can see the microplates inside instead of having to remove them to make observations. Consider using a freezer that opens from the top. For the experiment, leave the door open and cover with plastic.)

Procedures

In this project, you will observe how quickly different groups freeze, and then compare the results between all the groups. The groups include

- Plain distilled water
- Water seeded with INP
- Water containing particulate matter in combination with INP to see if there is a synergistic effect

Before beginning the experiment, locate a coal- or oil-burning furnace and scrape off the black sooty deposits you find around the exhaust. Alternatively, scrape similar deposits from around the stovepipe of a wood-burning stove. Collect the particulate in a clean white envelope until needed.

Next, fill each of the two test tubes with 10 ml of distilled water using a graduated cylinder. Label one tube "water" and the other "water+INP." (See Fig. 23-1.) Place four granules of INP into the tube labeled "water + INP." Mix the tubes by inverting them several times. These two test tubes will be used to create four groups:

1 Control
2 INP
3 Particulate
4 INP + Particulate

Now prepare the microplate(s) by cutting a piece of aluminum foil slightly larger than the microplate dimensions. Place the foil over the microplate and press the foil down so it assumes the depressions on the plate. (See Fig. 23-2.) Each group uses four rows of 10 depressions. If the plate does not have four rows, you'll need to use additional plates. Label the microplates as you see in Fig. 23-3.

Use a pipette to place 30 drops (10 uL each) from the "water" test tube into the first group of depressions. This is the control group. Use another pipette to place 30 drops from the "water + INP" test tube into another group of depressions. This is the INP group.

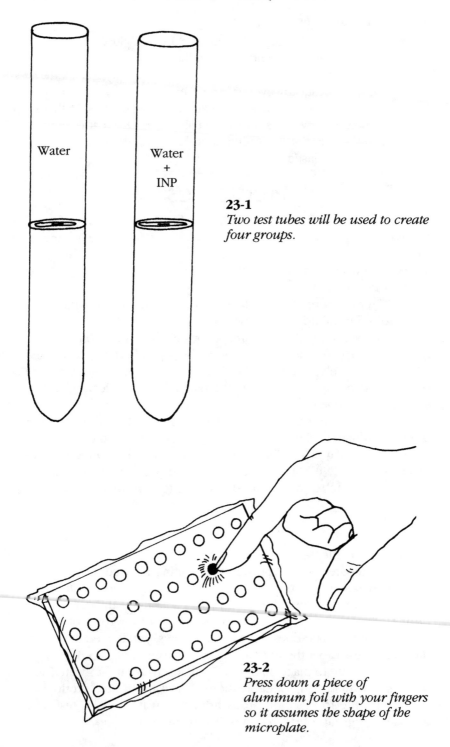

23-1
Two test tubes will be used to create four groups.

23-2
Press down a piece of aluminum foil with your fingers so it assumes the shape of the microplate.

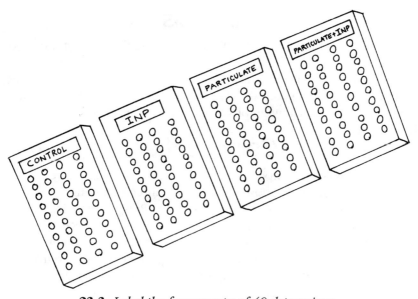

23-3 *Label the four groups of 40 depressions.*

Prepare the next two groups (particulate and INP + particulate) by placing a few small granules of the particulate matter collected earlier (now in an envelope) into the next two groups of depressions. It is important to keep the amount consistent among all depressions. Once this is done, use a pipette to place 30 drops from the "water" test tube into one of the groups of depressions. This is the particulate group. Finally, add 30 drops from the "water + INP" test tube into the last group of depressions. This is the INP + particulate group.

Before placing the microplates in a freezer, you need to prepare the freezer. Open the top of the freezer and place a sheet of clear plastic over the opening so it can be easily opened and closed. Also place a box in the freezer where you will place the microplates. The top of the box should be close enough to the top of the freezer so that the microplates will be easily visible through the plastic.

You are now ready to time how long it takes for each group to freeze. Place the microplates on the box in the freezer and begin the stopwatch. Observe the microplates every minute. Note when the contents of each group freezes at each interval. You might have a friend assist you, or consider doing each group separately. Stop when all the contents are frozen. Repeat this procedure so each group has been tested 160 times (160 depressions per group). If each group had 40 depressions, that would mean repeating this procedure four times.

Analysis

Once all your data has been collected, average the results for each of the four groups. Did the INP group or particulate group freeze sooner than the control (plain water)? How did the combination of INP and particulate compare with the INP and particulate alone? Was there a synergistic effect? Draw graphs to represent your results.

Going further

- Run the same experiment using a variety of particulate pollutants to see how each of them affects freezing.
- This experiment uses the natural (Ice-Plus) form of INP. There is also an Ice-Minus form of the protein that has been genetically altered. This form lowers the freezing point instead of raising it, and is used to protect crops from frost damage. Run a similar experiment, but use the Ice-Minus form of the protein.

Suggested research

- Research other potential commercial applications for both forms of INP.
- Study how and why INP is produced in organisms. What benefit does it give to the organism?

Appendix A

Using metrics

Most science fairs require that all measurements be recorded using the metric system, as opposed to English units. Meters and grams, which are based on powers of 10, are actually far easier to use during your experimentation than feet and pounds. You can convert any English units into metric units if you need to, but it is easier to simply begin with metric units. If you are using school equipment such as flasks or cylinders, check the graduations to see if any use metric units. If you are purchasing your glassware (or plastic ware) be sure to order metric graduations.

The following table will help you if conversions are necessary. (All conversions are approximate.)

Length
1 inch (in) = 2.54 centimeters (cm)
1 foot (ft) = 30 cm
1 yard (yd) = 0.90 meters (m)
1 mile (mi) = 1.6 kilometers (km)

Volume
1 teaspoon (tsp) = 5 milliliters (ml)
1 tablespoon (tbsp) = 15 ml
1 fluid ounce (fl oz) = 30 ml
1 cup (c) = 0.24 liters (l)
1 pint (pt) = 0.47 l

1 quart (qt) = 0.95 l
1 gallon (gal) = 3.80 l

Mass
1 ounce (oz) = 28 grams (g)
1 pound (lb) = 0.45 kilograms (kg)

Temperature
32° Fahrenheit (F) = 0° Celsius (C)
212°F = 100°C
To convert F to C use: $(F-32) \times \dfrac{5}{9}$

To convert C to F use: $(C+32) \div \dfrac{5}{9}$

Appendix B

Sources

Suggested reading

The following books can all be used for additional environmental science project ideas.

Byers, T.J. 1984. *20 Selected Solar Projects*. Englewood Cliffs, NJ: Prentice-Hall, Inc.

Gutnik, Martin J. 1991. *Experiments that Explore Oil Spills*. Brookfield, CT: Millbrook Press.

Gutnik, Martin J. 1991. *Experiments that Explore the Greenhouse Effect*. Brookfield, CT: Millbrook Press.

Gutnik, Martin J. 1992. *Experiments that Explore Acid Rain*. Brookfield, CT: Millbrook Press.

Gutnik, Martin J. 1992. *Experiments that Explore Recycling*. Brookfield, CT: Millbrook Press.

Although not specifically about environmental science, many of the following books have experiments that can be modified (with a little imagination).

Berman, William. 1986. *Exploring with Probe and Scalpel: How to Dissect; Special Projects for Advanced Studies*. New York: Prentice-Hall Press.

Bochinski, Julianne. 1991. *The Complete Handbook of Science Fair Projects*. New York: Wiley & Sons, Inc.

Irtz, Maxine. 1991. *Blue-Ribbon Science Fair Projects*. Blue Ridge Summit, PA: TAB Books.

Witherspoon, James D. 1993. *From Field to Lab: 200 Life Science Experiments for the Amateur Biologist*. Blue Ridge Summit, PA: TAB Books.

For an overview of environmental science terms and topics, try

Dashefsky, H. Steven. 1993. *Environmental Literacy*. NY: Random House.

For in-depth, college-level textbooks on environmental science try any of these books:

Arms, Karen. 1990. *Environmental Science*. Philadelphia: Saunders College Publishing.

Enger, Eldon and Bradley Smith. 1991. *Environmental Science: A Study of Interrelationships*. Dubuque, IA: W.C. Brown Publishing.

Kaufman, Donald and Cecilia Franz. 1993. *Biosphere 2000: Protecting Our Global Environment*. NY: HarperCollins College Publishing.

Miller, G. Tyler. 1991. *Environmental Science: Sustaining the Earth*. Belmont, CA: Wadsworth Publishing.

If you are new to science fairs, the following are a few good books to read. They cover all aspects of entering a science fair, from getting started to statistical analysis.

Bombaugh, Ruth. 1990. *Science Fair Success*. Hillside, NJ: Enslow Publishers.

Irtz, Maxine. 1987. *Science Fair: Developing a Successful and Fun Project*. Blue Ridge Summit, PA: TAB Books.

Tocci, Salvatore. 1986. *How to Do a Science Fair Project*. New York: Franklin Watts.

The following are insect field guides to help you identify insects collected for selected projects in this book:

Arnett, R. and R. Jacques. 1981. *Simon & Schuster's Guide to Insects*. NY: Simon & Schuster.

Audubon Society and L. Milne. 1980. *The Audubon Society Field Guide to North American Insects and Spiders.* NY: Knopf.

Bland, R.G. and H.E. Jacques. 1978. *How to Know the Insects.* Dubuque, Iowa: W.C. Brown Company.

Borror, D.J. and D.M. DeLong. 1970. *A Field Guide to the Insects.* Peterson Field Guide. Boston: Houghton Mifflin.

Borror, D.J. and R.E. White. 1970. *A Field Guide to the Insects of America North of Mexico.* Boston: Houghton Mifflin.

Dashefsky, H.S. and J.G. Stoffolano. 1977. *A Tutorial Guide to the Insect Orders.* Minneapolis: Burgess Publishing Company.

Zim, H.S. and C. Cottam. 1951. *Insects: A Guide to Familiar American Insects.* NY: Simon & Schuster.

For field guides that specialize in aquatic insects, try one of these.

Lehmkuhl, D.M. 1979. *How to Know the Aquatic Insects.* Dubuque, Iowa: W.C. Brown Company.

McCafferty, W.P. 1982. *Aquatic Entomology.* NY: Jones & Bartlett.

For information about the International Science and Engineering Fairs and valuable information about adult sponsorship, write or call

The Science Service
1719 N Street, N.W.
Washington, DC 20036
(202) 785-2255

Scientific supply houses

You can order equipment, supplies, and live specimens for projects in this book from these companies. For your convenience, a list of catalog order numbers from Ward's Scientific Supply is listed in this appendix, according to the chapters in this book.

Blue Spruce Biological Supply Company
221 South Street
Castle Rock, CO 80104
(800) 621-8385

The Carolina Biological Supply Company
2700 York Road
Burlington, North Carolina 27215
Eastern U.S.: (800) 334-5551
Western U.S.: (800) 547-1733

Connecticut Valley Biological
82 Valley Road
P.O. Box 326
Southampton, MA 01073

Fisher Scientific
4901 West LeMoyne Street
Chicago, IL 60651
(800) 955-1177

Frey Scientific Company
905 Hickory Lane
P.O. Box 8101
Mansfield, OH 44901
(800) 225-FREY

Nasco
901 Janesville Avenue
P.O. Box 901
Fort Atkinson, WI 53538
(800) 558-9595

Nebraska Scientific
3823 Leavenworth Street
Omaha, NE 68105
(800) 228-7117

Powell Laboratories Division
19355 McLoughlin Boulevard
Gladstone, OR 97027
(800) 547-1733

Sargent-Welch Scientific Company
P.O. Box 1026
Skokie, IL 60076

Southern Biological Supply Company
P.O. Box 368
McKenzie, TN 38201
(800) 748-8735

Ward's Natural Science Establishment, Inc.
5100 West Henrietta Road
Rochester, NY 14692
(800) 962-2660
or
815 Fiero Lane
P.O. Box 5010
San Luis Obispo, CA 93403
(800) 872-7289

Ward's Natural Science catalog numbers

Many of the items shown in the "Materials list" section of each project can be purchased from Ward's Natural Science, Inc. Below are some of these items (by chapter in which the item is used) and the catalog number used for ordering.

Chapter 6
Almost everything needed for this project can be purchased from a pet store, except for the glassware, which can be purchased from a science supply house. If you prefer to concentrate on the experiment instead of on procuring the equipment, everything needed is available in one package, #87W0004.

Chapter 7
Everything needed for this project is available in one package, #85W3503. The package is designed for classroom use, but affords the student the ability to repeat the experiments for verification, and to advance the original studies. Please note that only certain varieties of *Pseudomonas* will attack the oil.

Chapter 9
The soil humus test kit is #36W5521. The earthworms and most of the other supplies can easily be procured, or are available in a package, #36W5700. This kit does not include the humus testing kit.

Chapter 11
The rye seed, inoculated clover seed, nitrogen-free nutrient media, and most of the other supplies needed for this project are available in the package #36W0889.

Chapter 17
For the *Turbatrix aceti* (vinegar eel) culture, order #87W2900. Every-thing you need for this project can be purchased in a package, #87W3500.

Chapter 18
The solutions can be created with your sponsor's supervision, or they can be purchased with all the other supplies needed for this project in a package, #36W5507.

Chapter 19
Plankton (algae) collecting nets are expensive, so try to borrow one. If you plan to purchase a net, however, either of these two models will work well: #10W0720 or #21W1240. The water samples along with the other supplies needed for this project (except the net) come in package #86W3056.

Chapter 20
For the plankton (algae) collecting net, see the previous paragraph. Almost everything else needed for this project is available in package #86W3100.

Chapter 21
The preying mantis egg case is #87W6360.

Chapter 23
INP and all other materials needed come in package #85W3501.

Glossary

abstract A brief written overview that describes your project, usually less than 250 words and often required at science fairs.

backboard The vertical, self-supporting panel used in your science fair display. The backboard provides explanations that describe the project. It can include the problem studied, your hypothesis, photos of the experimental set-up, organisms used, analyzed data in the form of charts and tables, and other important aspects of the project. Most fairs have size limitations for this board.

biocontrol The use of organisms to control pest populations (also called *biological control*).

biodiversity Refers to the diversity of organisms on our planet and implies the importance of all.

biological categories Most science fairs categorize projects according to subject area. Awards are usually given in each subject area.

bioremediation The use of organisms to clean up waste products such as oil spills or radioactive materials.

biosphere That portion of our planet that contains life.

collecting aspirator A device for collecting insects that uses suction.

community All the populations living within a specified area make up a community.

composting The process of decomposing organic wastes, such as leftover foods, grass clippings, leaves, and sewage sludge, into a rich, fertile soil.

computer modeling, environmental Using computers to analyze existing data to make projections about what will happen in the future. For example, computer modeling might determine what will happen to sea levels over the next 20 years if global warming occurs.

control group A test group that offers a baseline for comparison where no experimental factors or stimuli are introduced.

dependent variable A variable that changes when the experimental (independent) variable changes. For example, consider the mortality rate of organisms living in soil exposed to pesticides. The mortality rate is the dependent variable and the pesticides are the experimental variable.

dessication The loss of all water.

detritus Refers to decomposing organic matter.

display Refers to the entire science fair exhibit, of which the backboard is a part.

duff Decomposed leaf litter.

ecosystem Refers to the living (organisms) and nonliving (soil, water, etc.) components of a specified area, such as a pond or forest, and the interactions that exist between all these components.

environmental literacy Refers to a basic level of understanding that a person should have to make intelligent decisions about managing our environment.

experimental group A test group that is subjected to experimental factors or stimuli for the sake of comparison with the control group.

experimental variable Also called the *independent variable*, this refers to the aspect or factor to be changed for comparison.

fertilizer A substance added to the soil to supply nutrients required for plant growth. Fertilizers can be natural or synthetically produced.

food web A simple representation of "who eats what" in an ecosystem. Food chains show one-to-one associations, but food webs show multiple associations. In other words, a food web is all the food chains linked together.

fossil fuels Includes oil, coal, and natural gas. These are all nonrenewable fuels, since their deposits are not being replenished.

fungus Primitive plants that cannot photosynthesize their own food. Most are *saprophytic*, meaning they feed on decaying plants and organic matter. They reproduce asexually with spores.

gall, insect An insect-induced growth on a plant used for protection and food by the insect.

groundwater Refers to water found beneath the earth's surface. Only 0.5% of all water is groundwater, but it supplies 50% of all drinking water in the U.S.

habitat Refers to the place where an organism lives, such as an aquatic or terrestrial habitat.

habituation The gradual reduction of a response to an event such as a stimulus.

heavy metals These substances are natural elements such as lead, mercury, and nickel that are mined from the earth and used in a vast array of products and manufacturing processes. These substances enter organisms through the air, on food or in water, or are absorbed directly through the skin.

hypothesis An educated guess formulated after thorough research, to be shown true or false through experimentation.

indigenous Refers to organisms that naturally live in an area, as opposed to foreign or exotic species that are introduced from elsewhere.

indoor pollution Refers to a negative change in the quality of our indoor environment where we spend 90% of our time. Primarily caused by the excessive use of harmful substances in building and furniture materials, and poor ventilation caused by windows that don't open.

inorganic matter Refers to substances that are not alive and did not come from decomposed organisms.

invertebrates Organisms with no backbones, such as insects, crustaceans and mollusks.

journal Also referred to as the *project notebook*, it contains all notes on all aspects of a science fair project from start to finish.

leachate The contaminated liquid that accumulates at the bottom of a landfill, often leaking into the groundwater supply.

leaf litter Partially decomposed leaves, twigs, and other plant matter that have recently fallen to the ground, forming a ground cover.

mechanical control A method of controlling insect pests in which control is achieved by a mechanical means, such as using oil to block the insects' spiracles.

nematodes Also called *roundworms*. Small, unsegmented, microscopic worms found in most habitats in great numbers. Most are harmless, but a few are parasitic to humans.

organic Refers to substances that compose living organisms or dead, decaying organisms, and their waste products. Carbon is the primary element of organic substances.

ovipositor The external female reproductive organ used to lay eggs.

parasite An organism that lives in or on one or more other organisms (the *host*) for a portion of its life. The host is not killed in the process.

parasitoid An insect that lives in another organism (the *host*) and kills its host during the parasitoid's development.

parthenogenetic reproduction The ability to produce young without the fertilization of the egg.

pathogens Organisms that cause disease in other organisms.

peat Rich soil composed of at least 50% organic matter.

pheromone A chemical that communicates information between members of the same or similar species.

population All the members of the same species living within a specific area.

population dynamics The study of populations and factors that affect them.

predator An animal that eats other animals for its nourishment.

qualitative studies Experimentation where data collection involves observations but no numerical results.

quantitative studies Experimentation where data collection involves measurements and numerical results.

raw data Any data collected during the course of an experiment that has not been manipulated in any way.

research Also called a *literature search*. Refers to locating and studying all existing information about a subject.

scavenger An organism that consumes dead organic matter.

scientific method The basic methodology of all scientific experimentation, including the statement of a problem to be solved or question to be answered, the formulation of a hypothesis, and experimentation to determine if the hypothesis is true or false. This includes data collection, analysis, and arriving at a conclusion.

smooth data Raw data that has been manipulated to provide understandable information such as totals, averages, and other numerical analysis. Often in the form of graphs and charts.

statistics Refers to analyzing numerical data to see if the results are significant or valid.

stimulus An event that prompts a reaction or a response.

survey collection A collection of organisms from a certain habitat or area.

sweep net An insect-collecting net designed to be swept through vegetation to collect large numbers of insects quickly.

topsoil Refers to the top layer of soil, usually containing large amounts of organic matter.

variables A factor that is changed to test the hypothesis.

vertebrates Animals with backbones, such as reptiles, amphibians, birds, and mammals.

Index

A

abiota, 59, 157
acid deposition, 128
acid rain and algae, 128-134
  acid deposition, 128
  algae collection, 131-132, **132**
  algae, 130, **130**
  analysis, 132-133
  concentrating samples, 131-132, **133**
  further research, 133-134
  materials list, 129
  normal vs. acid-rain pH, 128
  overview of project, 128-129
  primary and secondary pollutants, 128
  procedures, 129-132
  water collection, 131-132
algal blooms, fertilizer and sewage water pollution, 123
analysis, xiii
  scientific method, 10-11
applied ecology, 6-7, **7**, 19-58
  bug lights/bug zapper experiment, 20-25, **21**, **22**
  composting experiment, 34-41
  oil spills and bioremediation, 42-49
  ozone hole computer modeling, 50-57

B

background information on projects, xi
Berman, William, 70
biocontrol, 144-152
  analysis, 151
  egg collection and manipulation, 148, **148**
  further research, 151-152
  holding jar, 149, **150**
  materials list, 147
  overview of project, 145-147
  parasites and parasitoids, 145, **146**, 148-149
  predators, 145, 146-147, **146**, 149-151
  preying mantis, 146-147, **146**
  procedures, 148-151
  Trichogramma wasps, 145, **146**
BioCycle, 12
biological amplification of toxins, 115
biological magnification of toxins, 114
bioremediation, 42
biota, 59, 157
brackish water, 113
bug lights/bug zapper experiment, 20-25, **21**, **22**
  analysis, 24
  further research, 24-25
  graphing results, 24, **24**
  materials list, 21-22
  procedures, 22-24
  project overview, 20-21
  tabulating results, 23, **23**
Buzzworm, 12

C

chlorofluorocarbons (CFCs), 49-50
chromatography, thin-layer, 26
composting experiment, 34-41
  analysis, 41
  apparatus for composting, 37-38, **37**
  bin for composting, 38, **38**

  further research, 41
  garbage output, U.S. average, 34
  inoculant, 38
  materials list, 35-36
  overview of project, 34-35
  procedures, 36-40
  recycling, 34
  tabulating results, 39, **39**
  temperature control, 39-40, **40**
"cool" energy sources, 92
Culicoidea, 23
Curculionoidea, 23

D

descriptive ecology, 6
Discover, 12
displays, science fair projects, 17

E

E Magazine, 12
earthworms and humus, 60-65
  analysis, 63
  further research, 65
  humus content of soil, 60
  materials list, 61
  overview of project, 60-61
  procedures, 61-63
  tabulating results, 63, **64**
ecological studies, 6
ecology, 2, 3, **4**
  applied, 6-7, **7**
  descriptive, 6
  experimental, 6
  theoretical, 6
electromagnetic radiation, 100-105
  analysis, 104
  bacteria affected by EMR, 101
  devices emitting EMR, 102-104
  extremely low frequency (ELF) range, 100
  further research, 104-105
  gaussmeters to measure, 101, **102**
  health risks of EMR, 100
  magnetic fields, 100
  materials list, 101-102
  overview of project, 101
  procedures, 102-104
  setup for experiment, 102-104, **104**
  tabulating results, 102, **103**, 104, **105**
electromagnetic radiation and PCs, 106-112
  analysis, 111
  extremely low frequency (ELF) EMR, 106
  further research, 111-112
  gaussmeter to measure EMR, 107, **109**
  health risks of EMR, 106
  materials list, 108
  MPRII guidelines, 107
  overview of project, 107
  positioning for readings, 110, **110**
  procedures, 108-111
  radiation fields from computers, **107**
  readings from typical PC monitor, 109-110, **110**
  standards for PCs, 107
  TCO guidelines, 107
  very low frequency (VLF) EMR, 106

energy experiments, 85-112
  electromagnetic radiation and PCs, 106-112
  electromagnetic radiation, 100-105
  solar energy, 86-91
  wind power, 92-99
environmental science, 2-7
  applied ecology, 6-7, **7**
  defining "environmental science," 2, 3-4
  descriptive ecology, 6
  ecological studies, 6
  ecology, 2, 3, **4**
  experimental ecology, 6
  getting started, 12-18
  methods of study, 6
  pure research, 6-7, **7**
  theoretical ecology, 6
environmental stress and earthworms, 66-71, **69**
  analysis, 71
  dissecting earthworms, 69-70, **70**
  further research, 71
  materials list, 67-68
  normal earthworm anatomy, 69-70, **70**
  overview of project, 67
  procedures, 68-70, **68**, **69**
  toxins in soil vs. soil life, 66
  tubs containing contaminants, 68, **68**
environments, 2, **3**
  problems with environment, 4-5, **5**
eutrophication, 123, 135, 136
experimental ecology, 6
experimentation, 9-10, 14-15
  scheduling, 14-15

F
fertilizer and sewage water pollution, 121-127
  algal blooms, 123
  analysis, 125
  cultural eutrophication, 123
  cups for experiment, 124, **124**
  further research, 125, 127
  materials list, 123
  natural eutrophication, 123
  nutrient balance of aquatic ecosystems, 121-122
  overview of project, 122-123
  phosphates, laws and regulations, 122, **122**
  procedures, 124-125
  tabulating results, 125, 126

G
Garbage, 12
gaussmeter, 101, **102**, 107, **109**
"going further" sections, xiii

H
heavy-metal contamination, 114-120, **115**
  analysis, 119
  biological amplification of toxins, 115
  biological magnification of toxins, 114
  bottle preparation, 117-119, **118**, **119**
  further research, 120
  materials list, 117
  overview of project, 116-117
  procedures, 117-119
  synergism, 114
  vinegar eel nematode, 116, **116**
How to Dissect, 70
humus, 60
hypothesis, 9

I
ice-nucleating bacteria, 157-162
  abiota and biota, 157
  analysis, 162
  cloud seeding, 158

  further research, 162
  materials list, 158-159
  microplate preparation, 159, **160**, **161**
  overview of project, 157-158
  procedures, 159-161
  protein, ice-nucleating protein, 158
  pseudomonas syringae, 158
  timing freezing process, 161
  water, differences in freezing characteristics, 159
Ichneumons, 23
in vitro experiments, 11
in vivo experiments, 11
information and supplies, 165-170

M
materials lists, xii
metric system use, 163-164
MPRII guidelines, electromagnetic radiation and
  PCs, 107

N
National Geographic television series, 13
new solutions to old problems, 143-162
  biocontrol, 144-152
  ice-nucleating bacteria, 157-162
  parasitoids, 153-156
New York Times, 12
nitrogen fixation and acid rain, 72-76
  acid rain effects, 73
  analysis, 75
  free vs. fixed nitrogen, 72
  further research, 76
  materials list, 73-74
  nodules formed by nitrogen-fixing bacteria,
    72-73
  overview of project, 72-73
  procedures, 74-75
  soil preparation, 74-75, **75**
  water preparation, 74-75, **75**
NOVA television series, 13
nutrient-rich water and algae, 135-142
  analysis, 139, 141
  calculations, 141
  counting samples, 138-139, **141**
  cultural eutrophication, 136
  eutrophic lakes, 135
  further research, 142
  graphing results, 137, **138**, **139**
  identifying samples, 138-139
  materials list, 136-137
  natural eutrophication, 135
  oliogtrophic lakes, 135
  overview of project, 136
  procedures, 137-139
  samples collection, 137-138
  tabulating results, 139, **140**
  wet-meadow conversion of lakes, 135

O
oil spills and bioremediation, 42-48
  analysis, 47, 49
  beach simulation in petri dish, 46-47, **46**
  culturing petrophile organisms, 44
  further research, 49
  impact of oil spills, 42-43
  inoculating test tubes with organisms, 44, **45**
  materials list, 43-44
  overview of project, 43
  petrophile organisms, 43
  procedures, 44-47
  tabulating results, 44, **45**, 46, **47**
  turbidity measurements, 44, 46
oliogtrophism, 135
Omni, 12

ozone hole computer modeling, 49-57
  analysis, 55-56
  chlorofluorocarbons (CFCs), 49-50
  computer modeling use, 50
  further research, 56-57
  materials list, 51
  overview of project, 50
  procedures 51-55
  ultraviolet (UV) radiation, 49, 50
  UV dosage recording and calculations, 51-55, **52, 53, 56**

P

parasites, 145
parasitoids, 145, **146**, 148-149, 153-156
  analysis, 156
  egg collection and manipulation, 155, **155**
  egg-laying habits, 153-154, **154**
  further research, 156
  materials list, 154
  overview of project, 153-154
  procedures, 154-156
  Trichogramma wasps, 154
petrophile organisms, 43
phototropism, 77
plant stimulation and growth
  analysis, 83-84
  cuttings rooting in soil, 79-80, **79, 80**
  feeding plants, 80-81
  further research, 84
  materials list, 78-79
  overview of project, 77-78
  phototropism, 77
  procedures, 79-83
  seismomorphogenesis, 77
  separation of plants, 80, **81**
  thigmotropism, 77
  touch and wind simulation, 82, **83**
Popular Science, 12
predators, 145, 146-147, **146**, 149-151
preying mantis, 146-147, **146**
primary pollutants, 128
problem statement, scientific method, 9
procedures, xii
project overviews, xii

R

rain-making (*see* ice-nucleating bacteria)
Reader's Guide to Periodical Literature, 12
recycling, 34
renewable or "cool" energy sources, 92
research, 8-11
  analysis, 10-11
  experimentation, 9-10
  hypothesis, 9
  literature search, 15-16
  papers, research papers, 17
  planning research, 16
  pure research, 6-7, **7**

S

safety tips, xiv-xv
science fair projects, 11, 12-18
  displays, 17
  experimentation, 14-15
  guidelines for science fairs, 16
  in vitro vs. *in vivo* experiments, 11
  judging, 18
  planning before doing, 14
  research plans and papers, 16, 17
  scheduling, 14-15
  "signature," customizing projects, 13
  sources of information and ideas, 12-13

specialists, interviewing, 13
  use of this book, 12
scientific method, 9
  analysis, 10-11
  experimentation, 9-10
  hypothesis, 9
  problem statement, 9
secondary pollutants, 128
seismomorphogenesis, 77
soil ecosystems, 59-84
  abiota and biota, 59
  earthworms and humus, 60-65
  environmental stress and earthworms, 66-71, **69**
  nitrogen fixation and acid rain, 72
  plant stimulation and growth, 77-84
solar energy, 86-91
  altitude of sun vs. efficiency, 89
  analysis, 90-91
  angle of sun vs. efficiency, 89
  apparatus for experiment, 88-89, **88, 89**
  further research, 91
  materials list, 87-88
  overview of project, 86
  procedures, 88-90
  tabulating results, 89-90, **90**
specialists, interviewing specialists, 13
suggested research sections, xiii
supervision, xiv-xv
supplies and information, 165-170
synergism, 114

T

TCO guidelines, electromagnetic radiation and PCs, 107
theoretical ecology, 6
thigmotropism, 77
thin-layer chromatography, 26
Trichogramma wasps, 145, **146**, 154
turbines, 93

U

ultraviolet (UV) radiation, 50, 51

W

Ward's Natural Science catalog numbers, 169-170
waxed fruits experiment, 25-33, **29, 30, 31**
  analysis, 32
  developing plate, 32
  development chamber, 29-30, **30**
  further research, 32-33
  gel plate, 29-30, **30**
  laws related to waxing produce, 25
  materials list, 26-27
  overview of project, 26
  procedures, 27-32, **29, 30, 31**
  ratio to front (Rf) values, **31**, 32
  reasons for waxing, 25
  solvent front, 31, **31**
  thin-layer chromatography, 26
wind power, 92-99
  analysis, 98
  constructing windmill blades, 94-95, **95**
  fan speed vs. efficiency, 95-97
  further research, 99
  materials list, 93-94
  motor mounted to windmill, 97-98, **97**
  mounting windmills, 95, **96**
  overview of project, 93
  procedures, 94-98
  renewable or "cool" energy sources, 92
  tabulating results, 95-96, **96**, 98, **98**
  turbines or windmills, 93
windmills, 93

About the author

The author is an adjunct professor of environmental science at Marymount College in Tarrytown, New York. He is the founder of the Center for Environmental Literacy, which was created to educate the public and business community about environmental topics. He holds a B.S. in biology and an M.S. in entomology and is the author of many books that simplify science and technology.